SAYS WHO?

Paul Verhaeghe is professor of clinical psychology and psychoanalysis at the University of Ghent in Belgium, and is also in private practice. He is the author of *Narcissus in Mourning, Love in a Time of Loneliness,* and *What about Me?: the struggle for identity in a marked-based society.*

SAYS WHO?

THE STRUGGLE FOR AUTHORITY
IN A MARKET-BASED SOCIETY

PAUL VERHAEGHE

Translated by David Shaw

SCRIBE

Melbourne • London

Scribe Publications
18–20 Edward St, Brunswick, Victoria 3056, Australia
2 John Street, Clerkenwell, London, WC1N 2ES, United Kingdom

Originally published as *Autoriteit* in Dutch by De Bezige Bij in 2015
First published in English by Scribe in 2017

9781925322231 (ANZ edition)
9781911344445 (UK edition)
9781925548358 (e-book)

A CiP record for this title is available from the National Library of Australia and
the British Library

This book was published with the
support of the Flemish Literature Fund
(www.flemishliterature.be).

scribepublications.com.au
scribepublications.co.uk

Contents

BY WAY OF AN INTRODUCTION

One of my earliest memories: I was playing outside, where a new windowpane stood up against the wall of my father's workshop. I broke the glass, and cried and cried, afraid of my daddy's anger. When he came home, he wasn't angry at all. That memory remains with me to this day, especially my surprise. Why was I so dreadfully afraid? There was no reason for it. My father was a kind man who rarely hit us. Why did I turn him into the bogeyman he had never been?

I was 30; my son broke a pane of glass in my newly built greenhouse. I was so angry that I shook him hard. Regret. And shame.

• • •

Secondary school, iron discipline. The boarding-school prefect systematically picks out the weaker boys for public humiliation. Everyone knows it. Everyone is angry about it. Everyone feels powerless to stop it.

Many years later. Our faculty board is chaired by someone who holds both power and authority and is not at all afraid to use them. To be fair, I must add that he uses that combination for the good of the faculty. During a meeting, he really takes our colleague X to task. Colleague X is in charge of the library, and nothing there has been running as it should for quite some time. Everyone knows about it, and everyone knows the reason: a certain librarian with a permanent employment contract who can't be fired for love nor money, and who likes nothing better than to throw a spanner in the works at every turn. There is nothing colleague X can do about it. Getting angry, I brusquely barge into the conversation — thinking of those years at boarding school, the powerlessness back then, but not now — and voice my disagreement, saying that if colleague X is to be held responsible for the library situation, he must be given the necessary powers to deal with it. If he can't be given that power, then he should not be given the blame. After the meeting, he walks up beside me, puts his hand on my shoulder for a moment, and walks on without saying a word.

• • •

When I was a doctoral student, at a discussion between assistants and 'The Prof'. For various reasons, I was in the professor's bad books at the time. During the discussion, I brought up a point I was particularly convinced of. When it was simply brushed off, I repeated it, adding that the point was being dismissed simply because I was the one making it.

Years later, I was to have the opposite experience: attention being paid to things I said simply because they came from me, not because they were right.

•••

My first faculty board meeting as a very young professor. I am as proud as punch, and think I need to join in the discussions loudly and stridently. After the meeting, a senior professor approaches me and says, quasi-casually, 'Can I give you a little piece of advice, as a colleague? At the next few meetings, try to focus on listening, and wait a few months before you speak up yourself.' The man has authority in my eyes, so I listen to what he is saying — when I was a student, he was one of the few professors who took their teaching duties seriously. During the next meeting, I realise that my pushy behaviour at the last one was both naive and stupid. Lack of self-knowledge. I am sure to keep my mouth shut for the next six months.

Twenty-five years later, I and my field of study are attacked in the newspaper De Standaard. *A very young postdoctoral researcher at a different faculty is the chief voice in criticising our research. There are so many errors in his criticism that, for the first time, my department gains the backing of the entire faculty. One of my colleagues asks himself out loud, 'Is there no one who can protect that boy from himself?'*

•••

At the ceremony for graduating students, called the 'proclamation ceremony', in the great hall of the university, a former student, now a young colleague of mine, came over for a chat. She thanked me for my lectures and said, 'You always have authority in the eyes of your students because you don't make use of your power.' I nodded politely, finding it well-said, and gave it no further thought. At that moment, she was the more intelligent of the two of us. Power is not the same as authority. I would not come to understand that until much later.

ONE
IDENTITY AND AUTHORITY

In my book *What about Me?*, I described our identity as a construction that continues to evolve throughout our lives. The decision to focus on the issue of identity was entirely due to the nature of my work, both as a university professor of clinical psychology and as a practising psychotherapist. In the years prior to writing that book, I found myself having to dedicate more and more time in my lectures on psychodiagnostics to so-called personality disorders — that is, problems with identity. But what was the cause of this sudden increase? In my practice, I encountered more and more people who were struggling with the kinds of existential issues that had previously cropped up much less often. Furthermore, I soon realised that those problems went far beyond the scope of my field and that they affected all areas of society, particularly school and the workplace. I found the explanation in societal changes that have given a new meaning to our identity. A meaning that makes many people unhappy.

In summary, my argument was as follows. Identity is

a process of construction that unfolds in the same way all over the world, but its contents can vary extremely widely. This explains why different societies bring different problems to the consulting room.

The construction of identity is easily described. Our identity comes about by means of two very different, even opposing processes. I like to use the term 'identification' to describe the first, because it comes from the same linguistic root as the word 'identity'. Another term for this process is 'mirroring'. Right from birth, our environment and the people around us (starting with our parents) continuously present us with words and images, which we adopt. These are the building blocks with which we construct our identity. This predominantly social process explains why people who grow up in the same society are more alike than they realise. Literally, *idem*, the Latin word at the root of both 'identity' and 'identification', means 'the same'. Without being aware of it most of the time, we are all looking in the same mirror.

The second process, separation, is the opposite. Even from a very early age, we reject a number of things that are imposed on us by our environment, wanting to make our own choices. This process is more widely known than the first, and with good reason. Separation is typical of two periods in our lives that often cause parents to ask themselves why they ever thought having children was a good idea. Toddlers learn two words very early: 'me' and 'no', which they like to combine with each other as often as possible. Known as 'the terrible twos', this phase sees its sequel in puberty, when adolescents test the boundaries by overstepping them as much as possible, and set out on a quest for identification models that are particularly objectionable to their parents.

Identification and separation aren't mutually alternating processes; they work at the same time, albeit with varying relative significance. We often observe how, as adults, some people consistently tend towards 'no', thus towards separation. They actively resist everything they're offered. Others tend just as systematically towards 'yes', thus towards identification. For example, such people will be quicker to follow fashions, and more broadly, mainstream attitudes. Most of us fall somewhere between the two extremes and, in the best-case scenario, make a reasoned choice between 'yes' and 'no'.

We have a pretty good understanding of identification thanks to the fields of psychoanalysis and developmental psychology, and the recent discovery of mirror neurons. Separation, on the other hand, is barely understood at all — despite its huge significance for what makes each of us unique. What we notice about these two processes is that the first drives us towards groups, and so towards conformity; the second drives us towards autonomy, and so towards making our own choices. This is an uneasy marriage.

These two processes determine the construction of our identity. The next question concerns its content — who am I? Rather than searching for all kinds of personality types, I choose to see our identity through the lens of four important relations. First, I create my male identity by means of my relation to the opposite sex and what it means to me. Second, I am myself by means of my relation to my peers (age peers, neighbours, co-workers). Third, I am also typically me by means of my relation to my own body, to 'myself'. I will come to the fourth relation in a moment.

The link between construction (identification and separation) and content (the relations) is obvious. For example, the way I relate to the opposite sex depends for the most part on the society I grew up in. The mirrors I look into are culturally determined. This is why our identity differs starkly from those in other cultures, which look into different mirrors and so have other relations and therefore develop different identities — sometimes so different that they clash seriously with our mirrors, and thus with us.

The cause of such clashes becomes clear when we realise that the relations are chock-full of rules and prohibitions — with the prevailing norms and values of the society we grew up in. The claim I made in my previous book, that every identity can be traced back to an ideology, caused quite a stir in some circles. But it is easy to verify, because the relations that make up our identity are never neutral.

This is very clear to see in our relation to the opposite sex, even if the rules and prohibitions have changed significantly. Who has a headache at the wrong moment, how do we share childcare responsibilities, and why are women still receiving less pay for the same work? Do we restrict ourselves to a classic two-way combination (men with women) and applaud gay-bashing with our hypocritical silence, or do we see the existence of other pairings (homosexual) or possibly even embrace the complexity of gender identity as obvious and natural?

Not so long ago, those who are other-but-equal were called our 'fellow men' and, in a different idiom, 'comrades'. Someone we somehow had to help, even if we didn't really want to. Now, things have changed. Do I work together with others in a close team, or does my own career take priority? Am I prepared to give up part of my salary for the benefit of the retired, the unemployed, and the sick? Do I pay my taxes to provide social services, or do I harp on about 'tax freedom day'?[1] Can I allow others into my intimate space, or would I rather keep to myself, afraid of any physical contact?

This raises the issue of the next relation within our identity: our relation to our own body. While in an earlier, almost-forgotten era it was called 'Brother Donkey' (impure and the source of sin), today our body is the source of constant worry. Is my nose too big? Are my lips too thin, my breasts too small? Is that wart maybe a malignant tumour, and shouldn't I get myself screened for cancer of the colon? Unlike the Catholic saints of yore, film stars have perfectly streamlined bodies — impossible for a normal person to come close to achieving, even with endless training sessions in the gym. This constant worrying about our mortal body is part of a general obligation of enjoyment, whether it be in the area of sport, eating, or eroticism. Brother and Sister Donkey must enjoy themselves to death; the carrot dangling before their noses leads them to the gym, the sports club, or the plastic surgeon, after a quick detour to the sex shop.

Our relation to our own body and our relation to the opposite sex have now more or less blended into one —

we use the mirrors in the gym just as much to check out other people as we do to examine ourselves, and this has also turned such places into dating sites. The underlying fear is that of rejection. Am I good enough? Do I satisfy the invisible standard that I repeatedly impose on 'myself' because of the judgemental gazes of others?

Through these three relations there runs an all-encompassing fourth: our relation to authority. There is a compelling force at work within us that constantly dictates how we must and must not be as a man or a woman, as a peer, as a body. This force is both a part of us, and separate from us. Psychologists speak of 'internalisation'— the integration into our identity of prohibitions and commandments that were originally external (i.e. stemming from others). These dos and don'ts become part of us — the part that is constantly preaching to us. Freud spoke of a *superego*, another ego over and above our actual one, and he saw its origin in a forbidding father figure. It should not be forgotten that this internalisation is also a form of socialisation: we comply with the social expectations placed on us. I may well feel like chucking in my job, telling my boss what I really think of him, and pouncing on a (much) younger colleague, but I don't. Something holds me back and forces me to work hard, to be polite to my boss, and to behave decently towards my co-workers. I do all this due to a force within me. Strange.

Authority, normality, and power

This way of understanding identity also helped me understand why we have so many problems today. The social changes of recent decades set up new mirrors for us to look into, and so we acquire different relations, associated with different values and norms (success, competitiveness, flexibility, individualism, compulsory 'self-determination') — all based on the dominant economic model, which has become known as neoliberalism.

It has now been more than adequately shown that this system is not a healthy one. On a social level, neoliberalism increases inequality and divides people into winners and losers. This is not only unhealthy, but also dangerous. As an ideology, this model causes feelings of guilt and fear. It also imposes a constant threat on individuals, and those who aren't successful are told that they only have themselves to blame. The current tidal wave of anxiety disorders and depression is a result of this.

Originally an economic model, neoliberalism only has such effects because its power reaches far beyond economic life, and now dictates what is normal. At the root of the word 'normal' is the word 'norm'. Those who are normal follow the norm; those who do not are stupid, outmoded, or disturbed.

In this way, my research into the nature of identity led me to another question: that of authority. How can Western norms and values have changed so radically in such a short space of time — barely two generations? How has solidarity become a dirty word, while greed has become a virtue, and pleasure an obligation? What authority and what power associated with it lie at the root of this change? How does it differ from authority in the past, and what kind of a shift has taken place?

Finding answers to these questions has been anything but easy; this book is the result of my efforts. I can already make one crucial point right now: no one possesses authority on their own, as an individual. Authority can only be held or represented on the basis of something that goes above and beyond the level of the individual. Authority is moral in nature; it is the compelling force that springs from a group of norms and values that a society uses to prescribe the relations between its members. Between men and women, between peers, and with ourselves. And with those above or below us.

Contemporary neoliberal norms and values differ starkly in their content from Christian norms and values. Christian morality now commands barely any authority at all — its compelling nature has evaporated. But it would be incorrect to assume that this means neoliberalism therefore has great authority. Despite its dominant character, neoliberalism has little moral authority. Rather, the compelling effect of neoliberal norms and values has much more to do with power than authority.

This brings us to the distinction between power and authority. They're clearly two different things, but they're not mutually exclusive. Any form of authority contains an aspect of power. Authority requires power in order to enforce desired behaviours. In this case, we speak of legitimate power. By contrast, power can function on its own, without authority. Might is right — or, as happens so often, wealth is right: I am obliged to do what another person says because he is stronger (richer) than I am. In this model, power is a characteristic of an individual and has nothing to do with authority.

Authority can be seen as 'having the say', although this makes reference to the way in which authority manifests itself within an individual. Traditionally, teachers 'have the say' over their pupils, meaning they can tell them what to do. The fact that teachers these days don't have much say over their students is a good illustration of the problems we now have with power and authority.

Many people who are unhappy with the changes that have taken place in society blame those developments on the loss of authority. Conservative voices complain of the demise of Western civilisation, and some place the blame for that on 'the foreigners', by which they mean Muslims — ironically, a faith community that embodies the conservative norms and values far more than the contemporary Westerners who complain about the loss of those very norms and values. I can't identify with such voices, but, at the same time, they also made it clear to me that the West has a problem with authority, and that this is something that requires further study.

Then and now

Such references to recent grievances might give the impression that problems with authority are only a recent phenomenon. This isn't the case; authority has been under fire since the Enlightenment. That's not surprising, since resistance to authorities is ingrained in our identity. What we do on an individual level — critically examining what others confront us with — we also do on a collective level.

Periodically, we collectively call into question the mirrors held up to us, reject them, and may even shatter them. After which, we set out on a search for new mirrors to look into.

The philosopher Immanuel Kant sees a link between a child's development and that of humanity. Just like a child, mankind is 'immature', and humans must free themselves from this condition. Those who cast off this state of 'nonage' acquire authority and the ability to make choices for themselves.

Kant lived just after the time when kings and queens derived their absolute power from God and were thus able to rule as omnipotent monarchs. Anyone who disputed the monarch's authority also automatically questioned the authority of God, and that was never a good idea back then. From the 17th century, a process of democratisation was gradually imposed in the West, including a separation of church and state. Installing a new form of authority has been a slow process, which has sometimes progressed in sudden shocks. The most recent shock is still fresh in our collective memory and is known as the '1968 protests'.

What's striking is that, at that time, the concept of authority mostly conjured up negative associations, from hyper-strict patriarchs, authoritarian school teachers, and violent police officers to dictators like Franco and Pinochet. Authority was seen as despicable per se, and it needed to be destroyed. An idea — rather naive, in retrospect — arose that humanity would be better off without it, that a community would organise spontaneously in such a way that was good for everybody. *Communes don't need rules; long live freedom.*

Such thinking is the legacy of another Enlightenment philosopher, Jean-Jacques Rousseau, with his notion of the 'noble savage', wandering lonely through the woods, plucking an apple here, catching a rabbit there, while at the same time satisfying his mate and raising seven rosy-cheeked children. Rousseau was a fervent opponent of modern civilisation and in particular of the city, which he believed could only serve to spoil the idyll. No wonder, then, that the ecologists of the 1970s liked to draw on his ideas. *Civilisation and technology are bad; authority is synonymous with dictatorship.* 'Back to Mother Nature' was the message.

Mother Nature. You don't need a degree in psychology to realise that the authority that people were so eager to cast off was principally associated with a mythical father figure, the dictatorial patriarch. This stood in contrast to the dream of an equally mythical matriarch, the loving, caring mother whose prohibitions are so gentle on the ear that we hardly hear them at all. The teat replaces the rod. It's no coincidence that the first anarchist movements, which rejected any kind of centralised authority, often made reference to a supposed original and 'natural' matriarchy.

These two opposing notions feed off each other. The father notion, if I may call it that, evolves towards an ever-increasing body of rules, which, over the course of time, lead to more problems. Yet more rules are then thought up in an attempt to solve those problems. *Guidelines for Deviating from the Guidelines* (once seen as the title of a book at a psychiatry conference) is the best example of this, I think. After a time, almost nothing works as it should, because everyone is so busy anxiously observing the rules without thinking about their content. Sooner or later, the bomb explodes and the pendulum swings the other way: authority and regulation become outmoded — *long live freedom; everything will sort itself out on its own.*

Initially, that goes quite well, probably because the coercive forces of the past, and the fears associated with them, continue to resonate. Until it's revealed that priests have been granting the choirboys a very special kind of absolution, parliamentarians have been fiddling their expenses, and middle-class teenagers merrily join in the looting during street riots. And then the pendulum swings back again.

This is the direction which is once again gaining ground, namely a call for more authority — the very thing we wanted to cast off, not so very long ago. Back then, psychotherapists ascribed practically any kind of mental disorder to the effects of overly authoritarian fathers, so it was clear that those fathers needed to be removed. Today, we hear the opposite, and there are even some psychoanalysts who advocate restoring fathers to all their authoritarian glory.

The popularity of this attitude becomes clear whenever elections are in the offing. As soon as a political party promises to restore 'law and order', its opinion-poll ratings shoot up, and even more so if it can present a paternalistic figurehead as its leader. Just as remarkable is the fact that not a single one of those parties is ever able to keep its promise. Let's not forget that in this mindset, authority must always work from the top down: God the Father, the fathers of the nation (fatherland!), and those who represent them. You and I are not considered able to control ourselves. We are bad and weak, in need of upbringing.

Upbringing and authority

Ghent, late September 2014, a Thursday night. A horde of 18-year-old students staggers down the Kattenberg (a street near the Ghent University Faculty of Arts and Philosophy). Clearly first-years, they've also clearly been enjoying just a little too much of their new-found 'freedom'. The street is full of rubbish bags, and one of the youngsters starts playing football with them. The others eagerly join in, and before long the pavement is strewn with tin cans, squashed plastic bottles, and other trash. A 60-year-old woman happens upon the spectacle — she lives nearby — flies into a rage, and gives them a dressing down. Most of them take to their heels, but a small group remains behind, stunned by her outburst. The woman orders them to wait where they are, goes home, comes back with a roll of bin bags under her arm, and tells them to clean up the mess they have made. Then she leaves. The next morning, the street is spick and span. After telling me the story, she adds with a smile, 'They came face to face with their own mother.'

Mothers have power and provide safety. Psychologists often speak of children's secure or insecure attachment to their mothers. This is indeed of great importance and is closely connected to the relationship between mother and baby, far into the child's preschool years. Fathers do not usually become important until later. Paradoxically, the extent to which children are securely attached to their mothers can literally be measured by the extent to which the mother is able to let go of them. The following is a typical description of secure attachment behaviour. A toddler who finds himself in an unfamiliar space with his mother spontaneously explores his environment. Whenever he approaches a potentially dangerous object and his mother makes warning noises, he looks round with a broad grin and begins to move away from her as fast as he can, nappy wobbling from side to side as he goes ('Catch me if you can!'). This behaviour stands in sharp contrast to that of an insecurely attached toddler in the same situation, who clings on to Mummy's skirts and can't be persuaded to leave her side for anything.

We can measure the success of our parenting by our children's ability to leave us.

The extent to which a child feels secure has everything to do with his or her repeated and predictable experiences of safety as a toddler, which can have significant effects even into adulthood. People gain *self*-confidence because during their childhood they have the experience that they can trust others. Children learn to feel safe when they're certain that Mummy's disappearances and reappearances are predictable in nature. A mother who desperately tries to be present everywhere and all the time will primarily pass on her own feelings of insecurity and fear to her child.

We can measure the success of our upbringing by the way we deal with absence.

In this way, a nice symmetry appears. Some years later, mothers must learn to deal with the absence of their young adult sons or daughters, and need to be confident that they will return. Whenever children fail to leave the family home, or are forced to flee it, something is wrong.

Both reactions result from a history of insecurity. The root causes are diverse: unpredictable parents, an overbearing mother, a traumatic childhood ... When a grown-up child stays at home, it's the external world which is perceived as dangerous and threatening. If a young adult wants to get as far away as possible from home, the threat is seen as lying in the interior world. Those in the first group are clearly dependent, and solve the problem of insecurity by conforming. Those in the second group appear more autonomous and independent — until we realise they have an almost compulsive need to oppose their environment. The first group mutters a hesitant 'yes', while the second shouts out a loud 'no', and each ascribes an omnipotence to the 'other', which calls for either submission or resistance.

Omnipotence? The way authority sneaks into the processes of our early upbringing is easy to understand. A toddler is completely dependent on her mother, and will be prepared to do almost anything to stay in her mother's favour. If little Luce is a good girl, Mummy is happy. If she is naughty, Mummy gets angry. Thanks to a typical characteristic of human beings — our phenomenal ability to learn — toddlers soon understand how they're expected to behave. The first punishment a child experiences is the same the world over: removal from the secure proximity of the group ('Go stand in the corner!'). Even in the adult world, this remains the social sanction par excellence — namely: exclusion, imprisonment, exile.

Authority, especially that of the mother, instils in a child the security that enables him or her to become independent and explore the outside world without fear. This is an example of what Goethe described when he wrote:

> In constraint the master is revealed
> And law alone can set us free.[2]

Freedom, in this case, to go exploring in complete safety. Ironically, this security, acquired by means of authority, results in the fact that the first punishment (removal) loses its effectiveness with time — 'Go to your room!' 'Great, there's nowhere else I'd rather be right now!' — and creates a new challenge to authority. A child can demand autonomy far too early and far too much while her environment still expects her to conform to the demands of the group. In a traditional family, this is the moment when paternal authority is called in. In its old-fashioned version, this usually works in a rather less subtle way than maternal authority, because it is based more on physical power than on authority: ranging from shouting to spanking.

Insecure parents, insecure children

In a child's upbringing, safety takes precedence over freedom. As I was writing this section, I heard the following story about two young parents. They were tearing their hair out over which primary school to send their daughter to. They had visited various schools together with

Eva (just turned three), and now they wanted to know which one their daughter preferred. The toddler could not make her mind up; nor could her parents.

Eva's indecision reflected her parents' insecurity, and that's not good for the little Evas of our time. Today, parents' control over their children is anything but taken for granted. That children today are more assertive and more brutal than they used to be is only half the truth. This so-called assertiveness among children is a product of their parents' fear of assuming the parental role, which is one of authority. Their fear flows from ill-understood, though undoubtedly well-intentioned, pedagogical principles, along the lines of 'children should have a say'. However, what we forget is that these are children, that parents remain responsible for their children, and that no matter how much say children are given, their parents must always have the final word.

To believe that authority has no place in a child's upbringing is a huge mistake. As one young father said to me recently, 'I'm not a fan of democracy with five-year-olds.' Under normal developmental circumstances, parents are in a clear position of authority over their small children, and allow their offspring to gain independence gradually until they achieve 'majority'. Nowadays, we often reverse that natural order. Toddlers are allowed to do more or less anything (and are applauded for it), and few boundaries are set at primary school. When children reach puberty and begin inevitably to cause trouble, we try to reach 'deals' with them. This turns into a monumental disaster as we have failed to lay the foundations for such 'deals', and the problems just go from bad to worse.

It's no wonder, then, that schools have such a hard time. School occupies a position somewhere between the home environment and the outside world, between childhood and adulthood, between initial obedience and growing independence, and its task is both to impart knowledge and to form and shape young human beings. Parents these days demand that schools teach their children about authority. But schools complain that parents no longer take responsibility for raising their own children. So what is going on?

Education and authority

Increasing numbers of children are becoming problem students at school, while more and more schoolteachers find themselves unable to carry on working due to burnout syndrome. Problems with the education system continue to grow, and practically everyone has an explanation (too much modernisation, too little funding, too many immigrant students, too little orientation to the labour market, too many women teachers — even too many artificial colours and preservatives in children's diets). I believe the most important reason is the loss of authority traditionally invested in the position of the schoolteacher.

In the West, our tradition goes back to the Romans, when a *discipulus*, a pupil, acquired *disciplinia*. This meant knowledge and education, but also discipline as we understand it, received at the hands of a *magister*, a master. The master was older and knew better; the pupil was younger and far less knowledgeable. This difference meant the pupil must listen to the figure who was invested with authority by society. The intention was that, in the course of time, the pupil would no longer need the teacher and would be able to make his own way in life. In the medieval hierarchy, a boy would begin as a pupil or apprentice, later became a journeyman, and eventually develop into a master himself.

Currently, many schools are most concerned with being convivial places to attend, and education policy is often based on a supposed partnership between pupils and teachers. In this approach, the focus is placed on independent learning, as children are supposed to develop an appetite for education spontaneously. This means today's teachers take on the role of facilitator or coach — someone who doesn't need to exercise authority since, if the learning environment is challenging enough, children will naturally turn to learning.

This does not turn out to be the case in practice. But not to worry, the all-pervading discipline of psychology provides us with both an explanation and an answer that allows us to cling on to this image of children spontaneously demanding difficult study materials. The magic word here is 'motivation'. Some children appear to be unmotivated, or insufficiently motivated, to learn, or even insufficiently motivated to attend school at all. Motivation is a mysterious thing, though apparently it's something that a student can have quantitatively more or less of (no doubt someone is already investigating a genetic cause for this). It's also something that the younger generation clearly has less and less of. For this reason, it needs to be supplemented from external sources, and that must be the job of the education system, surely? One fatal criticism teachers face is that they 'fail to motivate their students'.

The result of this is that the classroom becomes an arena where a critical child audience noisily heckles a highly trained stand-up comedian as she tries desperately to awaken at least some interest with her multimedia approach. The complaint that school students aren't sufficiently motivated remains nonetheless, despite all her motivational techniques and attempts to bring the material down to meet the students' level of interest.

The next to be called in are the therapists. 'Our son is unmotivated, he doesn't see the point of school.' But even therapists can do little more than wring their hands. The fact is that forced psychotherapy simply doesn't work. The increasing demand for it explains why psychological treatment is increasingly evolving into a thinly veiled disciplinary measure.

Another solution — again by way of the psychologist — is to look for an appropriate disorder, which, like a deus ex machina, will explain why Junior's educational achievements aren't living up to the high expectations of his parents. This is followed by individual concessions — concessions that all share one characteristic: a systematic reduction in the demands made on the child.

I've no doubt that there are children who have difficulties, who would benefit from extra help. Practically every study carried out shows that the vast majority of such difficulties are associated with social disadvantage, and especially with its effects on language development. Research also shows that the majority of the help provided goes largely to children from the middle class, where the problems are much smaller.[3]

Now, barely anyone dares to take up a position of authority in our over-regulated education system, although everyone's begging for someone to do just that. This hot potato is simply passed back and forth. Parents want schools to raise their children; schools say they can only provide education. Teachers complain that parents do not deliver well-brought-up children for schooling; parents complain that schools don't teach their children discipline. But whenever a teacher is strict and punishes a student, it's never long before angry parents are beating at his door. If a mother raises her children with iron discipline, she's decried as a tiger mother[4] and even accused of child abuse. But raising children with too soft a hand is also considered wrong, and in some cases local authorities have introduced regulations allowing parents to be punished for their children's truancy. Parents are punished for not punishing their children.

While it has always been difficult being a child, it's now very difficult to be a parent. The roles even seem to have been reversed, which is shown by (fortunately isolated) examples of governments encouraging children to censure their parents. This used to be a tactic typical of totalitarian states like communist East Germany, where children were explicitly expected to monitor whether their parents were exemplary citizens. In 2007, the UK Home

Office launched a campaign that used children to influence their parents' behaviour.[5] The issue here may have been beneficent awareness (sorting waste, healthy eating, safe behaviour in traffic), but this remains a troubling reversal of roles. And the fact that the power that children have over their parents is referred to as 'pester power' is hardly reassuring.[6]

The next stage in this power switch has in fact already become a reality: children abusing their parents and bullying their teachers. A study in 2007 shows that three-quarters of Dutch people believe modern children are too insolent, antisocial, dishonest, and disobedient.[7] The Hungarian-British sociologist Frank Furedi cites a 2008 study showing that half (!) of the teachers in England report being bullied or even physically attacked by their students. It's notable that many teachers don't report such incidents to their superiors 'for fear of a negative evaluation'. Teachers are afraid of a bad report, not their students.[8]

And that brings us back to square one, to the search for explanations and cures for the malaise that plagues education. The conservative remedy calls for a return to 'law and order', while progressive thinkers recoil at that idea. This exposes a strange fact. For whatever reason, authoritarian ideas are part of a conservative philosophy, and anti-authoritarian attitudes are at home in progressive movements, such as those we saw in the third quarter of the last century.

Anti-authoritarian movements

In this time when conservativism reigns supreme, many people take a condescending view of that period, reducing it to the phrase 'May '68', a reference to the student uprisings in Paris during that month. Roads were torn up, endless so-called action committees were established, and some very famous slogans ('It is forbidden to forbid!') were coined. Reducing those events to 'May '68' ignores the fact that similar uprisings against top-down authority were taking place all over Europe at the time. From a historical standpoint, 'May '68' is little more than an exclamation mark in a story that covers far more movements than just university-educated discontent, and which began much earlier — with the radical freethinkers of the Enlightenment.

In retrospect, it's easier to distinguish those different movements: the sexual revolution ('Make love, not war'), anti-authoritarian education ('Freedom to learn'), liberation theology (Jesus as Che Guevara), second-wave feminism ('A woman's right to choose'), and anti-psychiatry ('Talk, not tablets').[*]

It doesn't take much imagination to recognise in all these movements the central relations that define our identity: our relation to the opposite sex, to our supposed peers, to our own bodies, to authority. This is most obvious in the case of the sexual revolution, since sexuality is

---

[*] These developments refer to Western societies, as does everything I write in this book. When that isn't the case, or when I wish to refer to a specific country, I point this out explicitly in the text.

connected to all these areas, whether we like it or not. How should I relate to my own body, to another person's body, and what pleasures are allowed? Why are women considered inferior to men? And why should I obey a person in a position of authority (teacher, boss, priest), even if his intentions towards me are clearly not benign?

The changes that took place at that time throughout these very diverse movements have had a radical effect on who we are now. The essence of this lies in the one demand that is common to all those protest movements: the call for more autonomy, for a move away from the 'father knows best' model. The coercive nature of patriarchal society created an all-pervading conformity, even down to the way in which resistance to that very system was expressed. Thus, as a student, I took to the streets along with hundreds of others to march against the obligation to keep in step. With almost everyone wearing identical brown parkas and the same blue jeans, we marched in step for the right to be different, and shouted slogans at a group of our peers who were also wearing a uniform, albeit an official one (and we had no batons).

As is often the case with social revolutions, a process of overcorrection followed. Paradoxically, the 'liberation' achieved was expressed in terms of 'must'; everything that was previously forbidden was now obligatory — it 'must be allowed', with the emphasis once again on *must*. We're currently seeing the opposite development. We have zero tolerance for many offences, a stifling culture of political correctness prevails, and many university students hardly dare open their mouths to speak — they are afraid, without really knowing what they're afraid of. And they have no idea who to turn to for help with their fears.

This is the challenge we now face: both as a society and as individuals, we have a huge problem with authority. For many, the solution is the return of a strong authority figure who keeps everyone in their rightful place, a cross between Dirty Harry, RoboCop, and Gandalf.

That solution will not work. As a cure, it's worse than the disease, and contains within it a return to self-imposed disempowerment. Kant would be spinning in his grave. If we want a real solution, we must first understand the problem.

TWO

AUTHORITY AND ORIGIN: 'WHY? BECAUSE I SAY SO!'

These days, a teacher who doesn't command authority in the classroom will soon be confronted with the question, 'Who do you think you are, anyway?' This is a very existential question, although the student who poses it has no idea how much his challenge hits at the very core of the problem. What is the foundation for that teacher's authority? What makes us respect one person's authority and reject another's? Or, more broadly, what exactly is the basis for authority?[1]

Defining authority isn't easy. One possible approach is to define it in terms of the difference between authority and power. In the animal world, authority and power are the same thing. The strongest animal has the most power, and the weakest has the least. The human equivalent is money: those who have the most money have the most power, and vice versa. However, in human society, possessing physical power and large amounts of money aren't an automatic guarantee of authority, much less moral authority. Indeed, in many situations, the use of power shows a lack of, or even a failure of, authority. A teacher who constantly dishes out punishments and must therefore regularly increase the severity of those sanctions has no authority. Authority is also not based on persuasion. A father who tries to convince his son to study more by promising all kinds of rewards, has no authority ('If you study for two hours now, you can spend the rest of the evening playing video games').

Thus, authority has its basis in inequality and allows someone to exercise power over someone else who does not question it and submits to it more or less voluntarily. In 1548, the 18-year-old Étienne de la Boétie wrote an essay entitled 'Discourse on Voluntary Servitude, or the Anti-Dictator'.[2] Authority has little or nothing to do with violence; submission happens voluntarily. A university professor gives a lecture and her students listen and take notes. A judge gives a verdict and the parties involved in the case abide by it. A doctor arrives at a diagnosis and his patients respect it and make an appointment for treatment.

The crux of the matter is in the above phrase 'who does not question it'. Why is authority seen as natural and incontestable? It's certainly not due to the person commanding authority per se, since this would be nothing other than pure power. The confrontational question I quoted at the start of this chapter — 'Who do you think you are?' — clearly touches on the most fundamental issue. The basis for authority must lie elsewhere, somewhere outside of the person who commands it. The phrase 'command authority' says a lot in itself. Authority is held by those who are in a position to express it (in the form of commands). A person can acquire, exercise, or lose authority, and confer it on others — thus the source of authority must lie outside of that person him- or herself.

The fact that the basis of authority lies outside the individual is illustrated by the difference between authority and power. Power is a two-sided construction and requires two people, for example, of whom one is stronger and can impose his or her will on the weaker. Power is always deferred violence. Authority, by contrast, is a threefold structure. A person commands authority over others on the basis of a third factor, namely an external source in which everyone jointly believes. It's on this basis that more-or-less-voluntary subjugation to authority rests. Authority is always an inner compulsion. If you want to understand authority, you must understand the basis it rests on.

Studies often refer to what is considered the 'natural' model of authority — namely, children's upbringing. In its most traditional form, authority rests with the father, in line with the observation that until very recently, every person in a position of authority was male.

At first sight, this appears to provide an obvious explanation for the source of authority. Fatherhood confers on a man a supposedly natural authority over his children, and so we immediately have a basis for authority as such. That paternal authority will then spread, as it were, to those in related positions (teachers, judges, priests, etc.), enabling them to exert a compulsive force to which people voluntarily submit.

This sounds like a convincing, if old-fashioned, explanation. It is immediately recognisable (fathers are everywhere) and, what is more, it alludes to a supposedly scientific argument (fatherhood is a biological fact; it is part of our nature). Yet to a critical mind, this answer is far from adequate. If fatherhood is *the* basis for authority, who or what is the basis for fatherhood? Answering this by referring to biology may seem plausible in these times of neuroscience and genetics, but there's no convincing scientific evidence for this.[3]

We see an essentially similar kind of reasoning from Freud, with his theory of the primal father. Every father exercises a naturally accepted authority over his children, as a biological and evolutionary legacy from an original primal father. What is less well known is that Freud himself eventually realised how absurd that reasoning is. So let's head off to Vienna.

Our fathers, strict but fair

Unlike modern psychiatrists, Freud devoted a lot of attention to the phenomenon of authority. Nowadays, mental disorders are disorders of the brain, end of story.[4] At the same time, we forget that psychiatry is the only medical discipline (discipline!) in which patients can be treated against their will, including 'mandatory detention', if necessary, in what used to be called an asylum. Confinement, in other words. It's no coincidence that the first psychiatric treatment was known as '*moral treatment*' — teaching people morals.

Freud describes his patients' struggles with their conscience over questions of sexuality and everything connected with it (which is a lot). In those Victorian times, the father figure was the embodiment of authority, and women and children had to abide by his paternal word. At that time, a person's moral struggle with their desires and urges was seen as going back to a struggle with their father. This is the basic idea behind Freud's Oedipus-complex theory, which he extended to our culture as a whole. Culture serves to hold our nature in check, with the father representing strict culture, and women and children representing voluptuous nature. In summary, Freud's Oedipus-complex theory goes as follows. A child — actually, a boy — is a jumble of urges, and dreams of removing his father from the scene so that he can have Mummy all to himself. Unfortunately for him, he must eventually realise that Daddy is bigger and stronger than he is, and he begins to fear castration. He becomes so afraid, in fact, that he sidelines his desires and starts to internalise those fatherly rules and restrictions, resulting in the development of the conscience (the superego). Subsequently, the boy's father does not even have to be physically present; the child feels guilty just for *thinking* about those forbidden desires.

Neuroses, the most recognised mental disorders at that time, arise when people try to be *far more moral* than they are able. If we follow Freud's explanation, we must necessarily assume that his patients' fathers were hyper-strict, and instilled the fear of God into them to such an extent that they were bound to become neurotic. This is also consistent with our image of the past, when men were *real* men and fathers were *real* fathers. And here we have our 'natural' source of authority.

As plausible as it may sound, the above explanation is wrong, and there are two reasons for this. Firstly, the image of the strict father is not reflected in the cases described by Freud himself. In four out of every five known case studies, we see a weak father figure, and it is the mother who 'wears the trousers' in the family. Furthermore, there is a second group to which Freud most often refers during the early years of his practice: fathers who do not abide by the law — quite the opposite, in fact. Sexual abuse was widespread then as it is now, and, just like now, the danger did not come so much from elderly male strangers. August Tardieu, one of the fathers of forensic medicine, reported as early as 1857 that the perpetrators of sexual abuse were often the victims' fathers.

So much for the *real* father: weak and a failure, or — even worse — an abuser.

Secondly, as I mentioned, there's a fault in the reasoning underlying Freud's theory. Exposing this fault will require several pages.

Freud: the imagined father

In 1909, Freud wrote the introduction to a book by one of his colleagues, Otto Rank. The book is about the myth of the hero, and Freud's introduction was entitled 'Family Romances'. In the space of just five pages, Freud describes how his patients manage to maintain an idealised image of their father. If their real father is too weak or — worse — abusive, they imagine a better version for themselves. *Pater semper incertus est*, there is always doubt about biological paternity. 'My father is not my *real* father. No, you see, my real father was a prince, a king. It was pure chance that I ended up in this family, a mix-up at the maternity hospital. I don't belong here, I know it, I feel it.' In a different article, Freud describes another common fantasy, in which the father is presented as the man who beats his child — which analysis reveals to be the expression of his supposed (again, imagined) love.[5]

The 'strict but fair' superfather is a figment of our imagination, created to correct the always-disappointing reality. The 'neurotic's family romance' described by Freud is a familiar leitmotif found in both blockbuster novels and serious literature, in which the real parents (who are never discovered until the very end of the story) are always different and, most importantly, better than their substitutes. We're probably all guilty of a more mundane version of this process: our fathers' qualities grow chiefly after they're dead. Little by little, we forget their annoying habits and exaggerate their positive traits as much as possible, which eventually turns them into people they never were. *De mortuis nil nisi bene*, do not speak ill of the dead. The most important thing for a hero to be is dead; it helps with the idealisation process.

The most striking thing about this fantasy is its persuasive power. Until relatively recently, just about everybody believed in the 'strict but fair' father, even though (or perhaps precisely because) the reality was evidently very different. Freud offers a plausible explanation for this: it is an escape into fantasy, a flight from disappointing reality.

But Freud isn't satisfied with this explanation himself. There must be other reasons why so many people believe in this fantasy.

Note that Freud also searched for an external source of authority, for a basic principle that lends a real, flesh-and-blood father his authority. This is the same question I posed at the outset. Freud's explanation has gone down in history as the myth of the primal father.

From primates to punishment

First, let me present the simple version of Freud's myth — simple, because it connects to a belief that's still popular to this day. Back in the mists of time, our ancestors — half-ape, half-human — lived in small groups in the savannas of Africa. Leadership of such a group was in the hands of the strongest male, who ensured law and order prevailed and kept the big, bad outside world at bay. But you don't get anything for nothing, and the alpha male's payback was that he could appropriate all the females for himself, and thus deny his sons any form of sex. If those sons became too presumptuous, he would drive them away or kill them. When he became old and grey, he himself would fall prey to his stronger sons, who removed him and then worked out among themselves who would take over the throne (and the bed). While this was going on, the trembling females would wait obediently to find out who their next lord and master would be.

In the second season of the HBO series *Game of Thrones*, we meet Craster, primal father in Craster's Keep, with his 19 wives, who are also his daughters. All male babies are sacrificed in the forest; all female offspring later share Craster's bed. Craster is eventually killed by the less trustworthy members of the Night's Watch, who also kill Mormont, their good commander, in the same action. They then go on to rape the women and plunder everything they can find. The moral of the story: rather a bad primal father than no primal father.

Such a story is still so convincing to so many people because it bears resemblances to the image that we have long been presented with by popular biology. According to this image, paternal authority is determined by evolution and is therefore a fact of nature that's somehow built into the DNA of the male. Thousands of years of evolution have fine-tuned the image of the father a little, it's true — culture, right? — but beneath every pinstriped suit and tie, there lurks a wild harem master. And women do so like to be dominated, don't they?

What's striking is how keen we are to recognise ourselves and our society in the animal world (the dominant silverback, the submissive female). Although, until very recently, that 'we' meant almost exclusively 'men in the scientific community', who — surprise, surprise! — consistently recognised a hyper-classical patriarchal model in the animal world. In this model, a strong, older man dominates a pack of obedient younger females, who are happy and willing to be mounted wherever and whenever the dominant male wants. He keeps rebellious youngsters under his thumb, and when they become too boisterous he drives them away. Certainly a wet dream for many a male biologist ... And, at the same time, a justification of the 'natural' authority of men.

It wasn't until the final decades of the previous century that this view was corrected, partly thanks to the work of female biologists (Jane Goodall's work on chimpanzees, Dian Fossey's on gorillas, and Birute Galdikas' on orangutans). Our close evolutionary relatives live in hierarchical groups, in which the leaders are not just leaders, but are also highly controlled by those lower down, in which females have much more influence than previously assumed, and in which individuals represent nothing. All behaviours are the result of social relations within a larger whole, in which the alpha male or female attains that position principally because of his or her ability to network efficiently and form coalitions.

Yet the pseudobiological tale of primal fathers still appears convincing to many people today, and some even point to Freud as the ultimate authority. The father of psychoanalysis did indeed write a story of this kind. But Freud's explanation is more complicated. Surprisingly, he places the basis of authority in an original act of violence *against* the father. Yes, once upon a time there was a primal father who ruled over his horde purely by virtue of his physical strength. Yes, he kept all the women for himself. And, yes, his sons did finally murder him, out of sexual frustration and a desire to take his place. But, no, his death didn't mean the end of his reign — quite the opposite, in fact. It was *after* his death that he acquired authority, on the basis of a subsequently introduced father cult. Rather than taking sexual advantage of the ever-available females after murdering their father, the sons fell prey to an all-consuming sense of guilt. Because of this, they raised their dead father to the position of a godlike authority, genuflected to him and made sacrifices, chastised themselves, and so on. In a nutshell, they became pious, obedient, and neurotic.[6]

The installation of the Law — in its most abstract sense, hence the capital letter — follows an original act of violence. In a later work, Freud would also see in that act of violence the origin of monotheistic religions. They are almost always paternalistic religions. Freud sees in their origin the same process he described in 'Family Romances': the son who raises the father to unknown heights and then subjugates himself to that fantasy image. In the most famous case, the son (Jesus) sacrifices himself to allow the cult of God the Father to arise and become established. The two other 'sons' — Moses in Judaism, with Yahweh, and Mohammed in Islam, with Allah — come off slightly better. All three establish the Word of the Father and an associated Law. Moses comes down from Mount Sinai with God's commandments written in stone, Jesus gives us the Sermon on the Mount, and Mohammed introduces sharia. The split between religious and civil authority did not come until centuries later.

Faith in the Lord

The source of authority is a deified primal father figure. Once worship of the father has been instituted, his authority spreads to all subsequent fathers, allowing them to become minor primal fathers themselves. This lends authority a religious and mystical aspect. From the primal father to God the Father to actual fathers is the general line of development.

This line of development is seductively self-evident, but it's based on false reasoning. Freud is honest enough to acknowledge the circular reasoning in his own argumentation. Every father gains authority automatically by virtue of the fact that he belongs to the class of fathers, going back to that one original primal father. But the authority of the primal father is instituted by the sons, and not until after his death. The absurdity of this reasoning put Freud in mind of a statement made by Tertullian — one of the church fathers (church *fathers*) — in his study on the nature of God. *Credo quia absurdum,* I believe because it is absurd. Patriarchal authority can't be explained by reason; it is a matter of faith.[7]

What becomes apparent, from both Freud's myth and the Bible, is that according to such reasoning, the source of authority lies outside of — and in this case, above — us; it's a higher authority. Moses came down from the mountain with the commandments inscribed on the stone tablets as the tangible result of his private audience with God. It is worth noting that in the original version, half of the Ten Commandments require the obedience of the faithful to the divine father, in combination with absolute and exclusive loyalty. Again, the reasoning is circular. God is the source of authority because He imposes on us obedience to Him and only Him. The rest of the commandments, governing interactions between people, acquire the force of law through belief in and submission to an omnipotent God — a power that must be believed in, otherwise it will collapse like a house of cards.

Pascal and the mystical basis for authority

In 1654, Louis XIV was crowned king of France. He was later to become known as the Sun King. He ruled as an absolute monarch and justified this on the basis of *le droit divin* — the divine right of kings. Following a religious experience that same year, Blaise Pascal — one of the most brilliant minds France has ever produced — started writing about philosophy. His most famous work is entitled simply *Pensées* (*Thoughts*). In Pensée no. 294, Pascal poses the question of the essence of power.[8] Even today, the answer he comes up with is as shocking as it is refreshing: the distinction between justice and injustice varies from place to place and from time to time; there is no mystical basis for authority. On the contrary, it rests entirely on custom alone:

> Custom creates the whole of equity, for the simple reason that it is accepted. It is the mystical foundation of its authority; whoever carries it back to first principles destroys it. Nothing is so faulty as those laws which correct faults. He who obeys them because they are just obeys a justice which is imaginary and not the essence of law; it is quite self-contained, it is law and nothing more.

Gulp. No 'strict but fair', no divine right. And it gets worse. In the next section, Pascal anticipates what Freud will discover a couple of centuries later. Anyone who embarks on a search for law and authority with the intention of finding its basis is in for a severe disappointment. There's nothing to find the basis of, and the more you search for that basis, the more fleeting it becomes. It becomes quite ironic when Pascal writes that the best way to undermine authority is to search for its basis. Freud realised this, too: seek the basis of authority and you end up with an absurdity you can't believe in. A deeply religious man, Pascal chose faith, but did attach a weighty conclusion to his sober reasoning: that this truth — that authority is founded on nothing but custom — should rather not be disseminated among the common people. Leave the good folk with their delusion, let them keep on believing that the Law is ancient and authentic; it's the best for everyone. Such a conviction forms the basis of what would later be called paternalism. The 'father knows best' model; the 'it's for your own good' model.

Pascal's Pensée no. 294 reflects a rare lucidity. Throughout history, basing authority in a divine body has been the rule rather than the exception. Humans ascribe authority to a deified figure, then draw their own authority from the very figure they have invented. This circular reasoning is found in what is both the oldest and best-known law.

A mere 4000 years ago, Babylon was one of the first empires known to have had an organised jurisdiction based on written laws. The Code of Hammurabi, named after the monarch who enacted it, begins with the announcement that the chief gods Anu, Enlik, and Marduk have appointed the king 'to bring about the rule of righteousness in the land, to destroy the wicked and the evil-doers; so that the strong should not harm the weak'. The king and his almost 300 laws have legal force because the chief gods wish it so — *says the king*. Thirty-five centuries later, the world's most famous constitution was written: the American Constitution. It had its origin in the Declaration of Independence, which, in turn, must also have had a basis of its own. What do we read?

> We hold these truths to be self-evident, that all men are created equal, that they are endowed *by their Creator* with certain unalienable Rights, that among these are Life, Liberty and the pursuit of Happiness. [my italics]

The Israeli historian Yuval Harari compares these two legal systems and concludes that the reference to God is their only point of agreement. The Code of Hammurabi is based on a fundamental inequality among men; the American Constitution posits a basic equality. Legal authorities appeal to a Supreme Being for their understanding of themselves and their laws as the only true ones. But apparently there are several of these Supreme Beings, and they all have very different ideas — with the exception of one opinion shared by all: that they are the One True authority.[9]

For us in the West, divine right is an outdated idea, and

certain Western Europeans may snigger when they hear the American president call on God for the umpteenth time to give emphasis to his words. We know better: we had the Enlightenment, that period in history when we discovered that reason offers a better basis for law and order than religion; and we can base our authority on that. Or so we think.

The myth of reason

A century after Pascal, Immanuel Kant, the intellectual pinnacle of the Enlightenment, made his appearance. According to Kant, the most important definition of the Enlightenment was 'man's emergence from his *self-imposed* immaturity'.[10] In the sentences that follow, Kant shows us the way to achieve this:

> Immaturity is the inability to use one's understanding without guidance from another. This immaturity is self-imposed when its cause lies not in lack of understanding, but in lack of resolve and courage to use it without guidance from another. *Sapere Aude*! 'Have courage to use your own understanding!' — that is the motto of enlightenment.

Kant's guiding principle is clear: think for yourself and become a free human being. The Enlightenment places reason in the foreground as a uniquely human characteristic. This reason is within all of us and thus everyone is able to use their intellectual powers to discover generally accepted principles for leading their life in the right way — principles that are generally accepted and as such no longer imposed by a higher power or its representatives.

I expect that most of us have at one time or another wondered how difficult can it really be to come up with a system that is just. And if that system is just, the overwhelming majority of us would submit to it willingly, wouldn't we? That would immediately remove the problem of authority and its basis. It would be enough if everyone simply used their common sense. The one or two exceptions who do not, would have to be convinced, and, if necessary, forced to do so.

The problem's solved, then, apart from two 'details'. First of all, no one can say with certainty what exactly reason entails. Second, any attempt to formulate universal moral rules ('maxims') betrays more than anything the limitations of those rules and the necessity of contextualising them. Much weighty scholarship has been devoted to this, but, fortunately, we can refute it quite adroitly. In his search for a foundation for morality, the Dutch-American biologist Frans de Waal offers two examples of classic basic principles, which he then overturns.[11]

The first principle is very familiar. 'Do unto others as you would have them do unto you.' De Waal: I spy a beautiful young woman at a conference, follow her to her hotel room and pounce on her (it's clear that this is a conference of biologists!). I treat her as I would like to be treated myself. When a vegetarian comes round for dinner,

I shove a steak under his nose, deliciously rare and oozing blood.

The second principle is really an extension of the first. 'What makes the greatest number of people happy, is for the best.' De Waal: A man is in the habit of playing the tuba all night long, keeping the entire neighbourhood awake, and will not listen to reason. He is (painlessly) murdered in his sleep, everyone in the neighbourhood is happy, and the problem is solved. By extension: a specific group of undesirables (choose your own!) is making the city unsafe, so stop their business and everyone will be happy.

The best attempt so far to devise a reliable principle of justice à la Kant was made by the American philosopher John Rawls, with his famous 'veil of ignorance' thought experiment. Imagine you don't know where you'll be born (Ghent or Kabul), who your parents will be (junkies or respectable citizens), whether you'll be a man or a woman, gay or straight, which ethnic group you will belong to, whether you'll be born able-bodied or disabled. You know nothing about the world you'll enter, but you get to choose beforehand which rules and laws must be obeyed by everyone in that world. Rawls believes this would lead to the fairest rules and, by extension, to the most just society possible.[12]

There's much to be said for Rawls' reasoning, but there's still the problem of implementation. If we assume that we could devise a just system of law on the basis of this thought experiment, the question of how it should be introduced into society still remains. It may sound cynical, but such a just system would only work if it were imposed, most probably by force. History teaches us that this is the rule rather than the exception.

Original violence

Kant's explanation of the meaning of the Enlightenment ('Immaturity is the inability to …') reveals two possible bases for authority. Its basis is either within the self-determining individual whose reason leads him or her to submit willingly to that which is best for all. Or authority stems from a compelling higher body, to which the immature individual submits. Both of these versions bypass a very pragmatic question: how is authority installed in the actual, real world? What is its starting point? Modern states aspire to equality and justice. But when and how did the modern state based on the rule of law begin?

History shows that such a beginning is nearly always surrounded by violence as an almost inevitable tool to overthrow an unjust order (Gandhi was an exception). From a legal point of view, it's important to realise that this original form of force *can* never be legitimate — quite the contrary. It necessarily runs counter to the existing legitimate order, and not uncommonly ends with the death of official representatives of that order. Yet it becomes the basis for a future legitimate order: an existing authority is violently overthrown and replaced by a new legal order, which retroactively legitimises that originating violence.

This is the conclusion reached by the French philosopher Jacques Derrida. After an at-times impassioned discourse on law, he reaches the same conclusion as Freud in his study on the authority of the primal father: authority always has at its origin a form of violence — that is its rather less mystical foundation. Law is law 'by force of law'.[13]

Even Kant has to admit this, albeit very reluctantly. For him, violence is never legitimate, except when used to install the rule of law. He sees the justification for constitutive violence in man's 'natural' striving for liberty, and thus as based on a law of nature.[14] Examples of this kind of violence are legion. The French ideals of *liberté, égalité, fraternité* could only be introduced by means of an extremely bloody revolution. The Founding Fathers of the United States were only able to write their constitution after throwing off the legal authority of Great Britain by use of arms. First, they were rebels (we would call them terrorists in today's parlance), then they were freedom fighters, and finally they were called the Founding Fathers. In Freudian terms: after murdering their father, the sons bring in a new legal order; after a time, they occupy the father's former position themselves and then base their authority in an imagined higher power, a mystical foundation. *God bless America. Gott mit uns. Allahu akbar.*

Back to square one: the imagined leader

In contrast to the traditional view that authority rests with God, and to Kant's conviction that human beings should think for themselves, many people believe that the best source of authority is a leadership figure. Faith in a great leader who assumes or is assigned authority on the basis of his natural qualities (he is wise and just) is a timeless idea. It goes back to Plato, with his wise philosopher king, but its most significant iteration originated with Thomas Hobbes. After him, Jean-Jacques Rousseau was to come up with a very personal interpretation, and, in early-20th-century Germany, Max Weber for his part argued in favour of charismatic leadership.

The English philosopher Hobbes grew up in a time when everyone was pretty much fighting everyone else. The Thirty Years War (1618–1648) between Catholics and Protestants was preceded by the war between Catholics and Huguenots (French Calvinists), and was followed by the English Civil War between the King and Parliament, Anglicans and Puritans. No wonder, then, that Hobbes wrote of the 'war of all against all' (*bellum omnium contra omnes*) and famously describes the life of man as 'nasty, brutish, and short'. As a political philosopher, he considered religion-based society to be a failed model and proposed a remedy that was unheard-of at the time: a secular society under the strict dominion of a sovereign (a 'Leviathan'), who is himself bound by certain agreements.

That last point — that the sovereign ruler is also bound by rules — is the tricky part. For Hobbes, authority had to remain whole and undivided — he was all too familiar with the bloody results of divided authority — and therefore it must be absolute. Hence his reference to the sovereign as a 'mortal god'. But the sovereign ruler must be authorised by the people in the first instance, in order to be able and allowed to govern. In this way, the people give up their liberty in return for security.

In Hobbes' proposal, authority no longer descends from heaven, but is granted to a ruler by society at the grassroots level. Two hundred years after Hobbes, Rousseau would publish his ideological masterpiece. In contrast to Hobbes, he argued for individual self-determination, for the freedom of the people to live in harmony with nature. However, with that very theory he also laid the groundwork for dictators like Robespierre, Stalin, and Hitler.

His reasoning goes as follows. All human beings possess natural, healthy instincts that drive them towards freedom and justice, but modern life (this is the year 1750) has corrupted them. The solution is for a Great Lawgiver to step forward and give expression to the healthy instincts present in every human being. In doing this, he expresses the 'general will', and thus no dissent can be tolerated. By virtue of his personal abilities, the Great Lawgiver is the best embodiment of the general will. His task is to (re)educate the people, so that they once again become aware of and recognise their own healthy instincts. Anyone who opposes the Great Lawgiver not only goes against the general will, but also unintentionally goes against his or her own best interests. This explains the huge importance of (re)education in bringing original opponents around to the view that what the Great Lawgiver wants is also what they want themselves.

In *1984*, George Orwell describes how the main character, Winston Smith, rebels against the totalitarian state (outrageous: he falls in love with a woman and begins to think for himself), and is subject to re-education to the point that he believes in everything he originally opposed. Orwell knew what he was writing about. He had experienced left-wing dictatorships at first hand. Even after the publication of that novel, Mao Zedong (in China) and Pol Pot (in Cambodia) would send millions of intellectuals off to the countryside for 're-education' and force upon them the freedom of 'a state … in which all dissidents are shipped off into "exile" or simply killed while happy crowds of healthy peasants salute the great leader'.[15]

The left-wing populism of yesteryear has been replaced by a right-wing variant, but the reasoning remains the same, and the great leader is seen as the mouthpiece of *das Volk* ('I say what everyone is thinking'). Indeed, in the early 20th century, the 'leader' — Rousseau's Great Lawgiver — lapsed into the 'charismatic leadership' as described by Weber.

For Weber, a German intellectual (economist, historian, jurist, and sociologist), such a leader represents the answer to a dangerous social trend towards a state that operates on the basis of rationality. The rationalisation of society lays the foundation for a depersonalised kind of authority exercised by an instrumentally organised government. That authority is exercised by means of what Weber calls the iron cage of bureaucracy. Such an instrumental rationalisation of society, writes Weber, leads to a separation of authority and moral values, and even to a loss of meaning. For him, the solution is to be found in a value-rational society embodied by a democratically elected charismatic leader. Weber defines charisma as 'a certain quality of an individual personality, by virtue of which he is set apart from ordinary men and treated as endowed with supernatural, superhuman, or at least specifically exceptional powers or qualities'. When such a person takes power by means of democratic elections, he or she can provide a counterbalance to the instrumental rationality and once again exercise a personal authority.[16]

Three decades later, just such a charismatic leader would take Germany into the abyss, and instrumental rationality reigned supreme. Hitler's rise was no accident. In times of crisis, people search desperately for solutions and place all their hope in such figures as Hitler. As soon as these leaders have been elected, democracy quickly disappears.

Hobbes' sovereign, Rousseau's Great Lawgiver, Weber's charismatic leader … It doesn't take a psychoanalyst to recognise in these figures the contours of the ideal father; and so we have come full circle, back to square one. It is no coincidence that Rousseau railed against bad parents and called for education to be restructured.

Clear-headed Hannah

The search for the basis of authority fails to deliver a convincing answer. Attempts to provide it with a 'real' foundation are simply unsuccessful, and even have the opposite effect. To my mind, the most clear-headed description of this stems from Hannah Arendt.

The life story of this German-Jewish-American philosopher runs parallel to the critical events of the last century in the West. Read her biography and — even better — her writings. In 1954, she wrote an essay entitled 'What Is Authority?' The results of her enquiry are as clear as they are surprising. In the West, the basis of authority is threefold in nature, and from it the power of persuasion has now almost completely disappeared.[17]

Authority is based on an external, superior ('transcendental') force from which someone can derive authority, but on the basis of which that person's authority can be removed. The concept of 'superiority' leads to the idea that authority functions according to a pyramidal structure. Those at the top of the pyramid are closest to the transcending source of authority and thus command the most authority. The amount of authority becomes smaller, the lower down the pyramid you go; each level possesses some authority — less than the one above it, but more than the one below. Furthermore, the different levels are firmly integrated and interconnected within the whole.

This results in a hierarchical model and reveals an important prerequisite for authority to function: inequality. Difference, in the sense of hierarchical difference, is necessary. Arendt delicately points out that the most egalitarian form of government is tyranny, with the tyrant ruling one against all, and the 'all' are indeed all equal. A crucial characteristic of authority is that it functions on the basis of voluntary submission. Tyranny, on the other hand, functions on the basis of force.

Submission to authority is voluntary since it goes back to an external fact in which the majority believes. For Western society, Arendt describes three highly interconnected sources of authority: classical Greek philosophy (Plato), ancient Rome, and Christianity. Plato stands for reason and eternal truth. Rome represents tradition and the ancestors. Christianity combines those two aspects and adds a generous portion of fear.

The way authority works is probably universal. Its sources, by contrast, are specific to time and place. This leads Arendt to conclude that authority as we know it is not an immutable fact. The authority we know came about within the context of a specific period and thus may disappear again. It disappears whenever belief in its foundation disappears.

The threefold basis of authority

In his blueprint for an ideal state, Plato places authority with the philosopher king, since he has the clearest insight into the eternal truths, into what is beautiful and good (*kalos kai agathos*). The masses don't have such understanding. In order to get them to act according to such insights nonetheless, Plato suggests a solution that still keeps the masses awake at night some 2000 years later. In one fell swoop, he invents both Hell and the immortal soul. The hereafter is a place where the final assessment interview takes place, with the gods as judges.[18] Those who led an immoral life are sent to the underworld, where they're punished tenfold for their wicked deeds; the good are rewarded and allowed to rise up into the heavenly spheres. From Plato's description, it's clear that neither he nor his fellow philosophers believed in this myth. And they did not need to, since they knew the 'eternal truths' and thus were able to lead exemplary lives. It was the ordinary masses who were supposed to believe the myth, so that they also would behave themselves, out of their fear of Hell and damnation.

Rome is the next stage in the history of the West. Every Roman villa had a domestic shrine to the *Lares*, the spirits of the ancestors. Authority could be traced back to the original founders of the city and their habits and customs (*mores*), which must be handed down from generation to generation. Authority rested on tradition (*tradere* means 'to hand down'). In the first instance, this was the responsibility of the *patres*, the members of the senate. *Patres* also means 'fathers', and the word 'senate' is also a reference to advanced age (*senex* is Latin for 'old man'). Due to their age, the senators were closest to the founding fathers and hence had the greatest share in patriarchal authority.

The definitive foundation of traditional authority came with Christianity in the fifth century AD. This is the period when the church took over political power and the 'Holy Roman Empire' was formed, in which the most important of the church fathers, Saint Augustine of Hippo, combined Athens and Rome. Hell as described by Plato became part of Christian doctrine, and sinners could no longer simply expect forgiveness, but rather most of them would burn in the fires of Hell. Eternal truth now lay with God, and the philosophers had to make room for true believers. From the Romans, Augustine learned the importance of the city, foundation, and tradition. Christianity's founding act was the death and resurrection of Christ. This act resulted in the foundation of the *Civitas Dei*, the City of God. A few centuries later, the Pope, as successor to the first founding father (Saint Peter), acquired supreme authority as God's highest representative on Earth. His blessing is *Urbi et Orbi* ('to the city and the world'), and Rome remains the eternal city.*

Thus the three founding elements come together: a higher truth, with God the Father as its supreme source; the founding act with its associated traditions; and Hell as the deterrent for the masses. This combination is so powerful that it has been the exclusive dominant influence for almost two millennia. Its most important basis is, without doubt, fear — fear of penalty and punishment, of eternal damnation in Hell or at least of an unbearably long period spent in the purging fires of Purgatory. For centuries, 'living in fear of God' was a reality that we can scarcely imagine today.

History is peppered with popes and cardinals, emperors and kings, princes, knights, and judges, all representatives of God the Father, and all 'blessed' by Him with an often-absolute authority for which they had to account only before God (and with which, in their own reckoning, He was always in accord). What Arendt strangely fails to

---

* When we speak of the 'origin', the 'basis', or the 'source' of authority, we are looking backwards and downwards, as it were. This is a legacy of classical Rome, with its emphasis on foundation and ancestry. When we place the source of authority above us, in a 'higher', 'transcendental' power, we are following Platonic and Christian reasoning. That latter metaphor in particular is dominant in our way of thinking, which is even reflected in our architecture: management executives occupy the top floors of an office building, while the porter has to make do with a place in the basement.

notice is that the threefold basis of authority as she sees it repeatedly reaffirms the patriarchy. For the ancient Greeks, the free citizen was, by definition, a man. Rome is the *patria*, the fatherland, governed by the *patres* of the senate. Christianity is the prime example of a patriarchy, with mandatory submission to God the Father and with women as the source of evil — unless they are mothers, and even then, they should preferably also be virgins.

What Arendt *does* notice in 1954 is that authority — or at least this traditional patriarchal version of it — is disappearing.

The disappearance of patriarchal authority

Every couple of weeks, I visit a man who used to be my neighbour. He's 84 years old and recently became paralysed down one side of his body, condemning him to a passive existence. As a consequence of his rural, farming background, the time he grew up in, and World War II, he never received much in the way of a formal education. But that's not to say he's any less intelligent than you or I. One of his recurring laments is, 'What a load of lies they had us believe!' By 'they' he mainly means 'the church'. He no longer believes in anything, including traditional politics — for him, these things have simply lost their authority. This is even truer of the younger generation: there's no hereafter, only the here-and-now, and an overriding fear of not having lived to the full.

The disappearance of the fear of Hell has undermined the connection between religion and authority. What's more, this is happening in a generation and at a time when the connection between authority and greater age has been wiped out. Tradition now serves mainly as a tourist attraction. We are abolishing the senate. Experience (seniority) is an impediment, and forget about trying to find a job after the age of 50. Companies, universities, and psychiatric institutions still pride themselves on having been 'established in 1817', but when it comes to their own year of birth, the managers in those places prefer to keep quiet. Everything has to be young, hip, and happening; old is out. And eternal truths may persist for just one more (fashion) season.

No fear of the hereafter, no tradition, no belief — for Hannah Arendt, the implications are clear. Authority as we knew it has disappeared, never to return. Arendt's work illustrates what we read in Pascal. Inquire into the foundation of authority and you end up undermining it. 'We must make it regarded as authoritative, eternal, and conceal its origin, if we do not wish that it should soon come to an end [that is, authority and the oppression associated with it].'[19]

That process of disappearance began much earlier, as evidenced by the question that Pascal asks himself. He also offers an explanation for why it has taken so long: humans are creatures of habit, and when customs lose their reason for being, they don't disappear immediately — they die a long, drawn-out death, although the process does reach a point at which it begins to speed up.

The reasons for the disappearance of religion and tradition are well known: improved access to education and knowledge for more people, combined with the pragmatic answers offered by science. We no longer pray to Saint Apollonia (patron saint of those suffering from toothache), we consult our dentist. And sex is now a good thing, not a sin. More and more people are gaining access to knowledge that has a strongly relativising effect; fewer and fewer people are afraid of the fires of Hell.

We have now arrived at a very sobering answer to the question I asked at the start of this chapter. Authority rests upon a belief in a mystical foundation and upon fear, against the backdrop of an original form of violence. It is always legitimised retrospectively as authority, which results in the appearance of a substantive basis for its existence. And as soon as we begin to investigate this substantive basis, it turns out to have no basis at all. My generation learned this truth early in life. As children, whenever we asked too many times why we had to do this or that, why we had to 'behave', the answer would be, 'Why? Because I say so!', usually accompanied by a clip round the ear.

A structural view of authority

Traditional authority is synonymous with patriarchal authority: top-down and the preserve of men. That link is so strong that we are barely able to conceive of a different interpretation. This explains the panicked nature of reactions to the disappearance of authority, and attempts to restore it. On the basis of Arendt's work, we can appreciate that those efforts will fail and that authority and patriarchy need not be synonyms. Her analysis allows us to lay bare the structure of authority and see how other interpretations are possible. As an important bonus, we also come to understand the difference between authority and power.

Authority is a threefold structure. (1) Something (an institution) or someone (an authority figure) commands authority over (2) something or someone else on the basis of (3) an external foundation that the parties involved believe in and to which they therefore willingly submit. This external source needn't necessarily be 'higher' (Christianity) or 'older' (Rome, tradition) and it doesn't necessarily have to work in a top-down, pyramidal way. But it must lie outside of the individual and be accepted by the majority. If these requirements are met, authority exists. Whoever or whatever commands authority (an individual, an institution) can do so because the majority hands him, her, or it control. If the person or institution no longer uses that control properly, authority is removed from them and passed to someone else.

Authority implies power and possibly the exercise of legitimate violence. Power and violence are only used on someone who no longer willingly submits to authority — that is, someone who breaks the law. When a majority of people refuse to continue to submit (because belief in the basis of authority has disappeared), authority collapses. At that point, what earlier was legitimate violence begins to function as pure power, resulting in an increase of violence and forced submission. If this situation persists, history has shown that counter-violence will arise — that is, rebellion and revolt. Often, a new authority emerges with time, which retrospectively legitimises the original violence.

What used to be just a revolt is rebranded as a fight for freedom.

We hardly realise it, but we are experiencing the end of an era. We're taking leave of the patriarchal form of authority that determined all aspects of our lives for roughly 10,000 years — the sexual, the social, the religious, the political, and the economic.[20] This doesn't mean that we're taking leave of authority itself. Arendt argues that society can't exist without authority, since its function is to regulate inter-human relationships. In the closing sentence of her essay, she notes that when authority falls away, we are once again confronted with 'the elementary problems of human living-together'. The key question is what new form of authority we should develop.

There's an urgent need to answer that question, since it has become more than obvious that traditional authority no longer works in a number of classic inter-human relationships.

THREE IMPOSSIBLE PROFESSIONS

In 1925, Freud mentioned a witticism that would turn out to be prophetic. The joke went that there are three professions that are impossible: *Erziehen, Kurieren, und Regieren*; educating, healing, and governing. In Freud's time, those professions referred to male figures: fathers, doctors, and politicians. In 1972, the French psychoanalyst Jacques Lacan issued a surprising statement: the feeling most closely associated with fatherhood is shame. He could have said the same about politicians, and, though it saddens me to the heart to do so, I must also add psychotherapists to that list. All three are doomed to failure, from whence the shame.[1]

To be clear: I am indeed completely convinced that parenting, politics, and helping people are possible. The impossibility that Freud writes about and the shame mentioned by Lacan have to do with a specific interpretation of those three activities, an interpretation that's inextricably linked with the patriarchal position of the master figure. Father knows best and he's the boss;

politicians promise everything will be different under their government; therapists brandish their 'evidence-based research' to show that the efficacy of their treatments is, well ... evident.

This system functioned for centuries for the simple reason that most people believed in it. In the previous chapter, I gave the following illustrations of the unquestioned acceptance of authorities. University professors lectured; their students listened. Judges handed down verdicts; the parties involved abided by them. Doctors made diagnoses; patients accepted them. Nowadays, lecturers have to turn up the volume on their lapel mics to be heard above their students' chatter. Defendants invariably appeal against their verdicts, with the full support of their lawyers (*ker-ching!*). And patients turn to other doctors for a second or even third opinion.

Once again: the patriarchy can only function on the basis of general belief in it. If the foundation for that belief disappears, then any master will have had his day. This is the conclusion of Hannah Arendt: an individual can't have authority alone, no matter what intrinsic qualities he or she possesses. Authority is conferred on someone by third parties on the basis of their belief in the underlying system. No one can occupy a position of a master on his or her own. The emperor is always naked until a child dares to point the fact out. In traditional patriarchal settings, that child gets a clip round the ear and learns to keep his mouth shut. No one must reveal the secrets of the crown.

The closer someone is to the master — father, king, emperor, but also university professor, doctor, or party leader

— the more familiar that person is with the weaknesses of the leadership figure. And, more often than not, with the weaknesses of the leadership's views. Only very few people at a party's headquarters believe unreservedly in the ideology they profess to the outside world. Yet until very recently, no one would have dreamed of publicising weaknesses, mistakes, or even deceit. Revealing the secrets of the crown was tantamount to treason, and, in the past, loyalty mainly meant helping to keep up appearances.

Such complicity is now more or less a thing of the past. The group to which the whistleblower Edward Snowden belongs is growing, and it's a good illustration of the extent to which society's belief in a 'strict but fair' father has crumbled. Note that the Snowdens of our time reveal information to serve the general good, often at great risk to themselves and not for financial gain, in contrast to ordinary opportunists. A tragic example of such a whistleblower is Arthur Gotlieb, who brought corrupt practices at the Dutch Healthcare Authority (NZa) to light. As a result, he was harassed to such an extent that he eventually took his own life.[2]

What's typical of our time is that whistleblowers are no longer isolated figures — WikiLeaks functions as a collective, which enables it to work all the more thoroughly. Who would ever have thought that a descendent of a ruler of the 'Holy Roman Empire', and moreover the husband of Bismarck's granddaughter, would be forced to resign as German minister of defence because he cheated on his doctoral thesis? Karl-Theodor zu Guttenberg had to stand down after a digital open peer review of his dissertation threw up overwhelming evidence of plagiarism.[3]

The disappearance of traditional loyalty — better described as complicity — means an ever-increasing number of scandals are coming to light, in the church, in politics, in education, in the bosom of the family. Abuse of power is structurally woven into the fabric of the patriarchal system. These are *not* random errors made by figures who managed to find their way into leadership positions when they shouldn't have. It's the leadership position itself that's so conducive to such mistakes.

Place someone in an unassailable position (unassailable because almost everyone believes it to be), combine that with a lack of effective outside control, and you have a breeding ground for abuse. A patriarchal authority very often creates a closed society, which views the outside world as hostile and/or inferior. In more extreme cases, such a society will even shut the door on the outside world completely. The more closed-off a group is, the more pathological it is — this is a lesson we've learned from clinical psychology and classical psychiatry. No one can enter an incestuous family from the outside, and no one is allowed to leave, either. In a totalitarian state, citizens have only very limited freedom of movement, and foreign guests are provided with a 'guide' who makes sure they only see what is allowed. As soon as this isolation is broken, the days of a totalitarian regime are numbered.

Incest is an extreme version of the type of abuse of power that arises in such closed groups. This puts me in mind of a statement I once heard from Karine Vandenberghe, former president of Amnesty International's

Flemish division: 'Why do people hit and abuse their family members? Because they can.' In this phrase, 'people' almost always means 'male partners and fathers', and 'family members' are 'women and children'. And this brings me to the first impossible 'profession': fatherhood.

Parenting as an impossible profession: the end of the father

There will always be fathers, as a biological necessity, so to speak. But the automatic and exclusive nature of paternal authority as we knew it until recently has evaporated as a result of the gradual disappearance of the patriarchy. That leaves us with a man-sized question mark, since parenting is simply impossible without authority.

Within traditional families, there was a very clear division of roles. The power was mainly in the hands of the mother, in the form of a typical two-way relationship (mother versus child). Authority lay mainly with the father, without his having to do very much to earn it — the source of his authority was outside of him. Mothers stayed at home, looked after the house, and had a very immediate relationship with their children. Fathers were distant figures who left home early in the morning and returned in the evening at a predictable time from an activity called 'work'. Father's return was not always a time to look forward to, because if a child had been naughty during the day, the odds were that Mummy would tell Daddy about it. And the consequence was often a spanking. A traditional Flemish nursery rhyme goes as follows:

Mummy's going to scold you,
Daddy's going to spank you,
Little kiddie, little kiddie, run as fast as you can!

The audience of Belgium's public, Flemish-language children's channel, Ketnet, heard a revised second line in 2012: 'Oh my dearest Mummy, please don't tell Daddy'. A spokesperson for the broadcaster said the old text was no longer appropriate for today's society, and added that the text had already been changed in the Netherlands quite some time before.

The new, so-called progressive version creates a complicity between two of the three people involved, to the exclusion of the third, and that's a bad idea for several reasons. Let's return to the difference between power and authority. Pure power operates between two individuals, among whom the stronger, by definition, holds the reins. There's no outside control, and power can be exercised arbitrarily. Authority, by contrast, presupposes a threefold structure, in which one person or agency can command authority over a second, by dint of a third. That is to say, on the basis of an external source, outside of both of them. And this has a very important implication: in principle, authority owes its accountability to a third agency. Parents are the representatives of rules and laws, on the understanding that they are themselves also bound by those rules. The power they hold over their children should never be pure power, and is limited by authority.

In the traditional family, it was principally the father who represented the law and the outside world. The mother would expressly invoke him ('Wait till your father gets home!'), and the father could then invoke the outside world. Mothers remained in the home, where they had a lot of power, but they barely commanded any authority. The authority commanded by the father was granted to him by law. Authority figures are characterised by the fact that they invoke an external source of their authority, without coinciding with that authority. Furthermore, as bearers of authority, they're subject to a wider authority, which also applies to them.

This brings us to the weakness in the patriarchal family of yore. Some fathers revealed themselves to be dictators, making up their own rules in their little kingdoms. There was barely any outside control, since the family was at the very bottom of the pyramidal structure that typified the patriarchal system. Those who found themselves below the head of the family had nowhere to turn. Those above him closed their eyes with typical complicity. The first safe houses for abused women date from the 1970s, and rape within marriage didn't become illegal until the 1990s.

From our modern point of view, it's striking how little the fathers of the past engaged with their children. For one thing, they were often out of the house, either at work or at the football. Moreover, bringing up children was not seen as one of their core tasks. Their interventions were mostly restricted to the signing of school reports and the meting out of punishments at the behest of the mother. Punishments were accompanied by a sermon in which the father would have a stern word with his son or daughter, invariably with a warning about the future. The use of the word 'sermon' shows the similar position of the pastor or priest, who — along with the schoolteacher — occupied the next level on the traditional pyramid of authority.

The patriarchal father was typically an absent father. This lack of presence increased his bogeyman character and served to prevent his failings from coming to light all too quickly. The patriarchal system gave fathers a superhuman dimension, and, as the embodiment of law and order, they were expected to set a good example at all times. The discovery of a father's failings then came as a slap in the face. Steinbeck puts this into painfully beautiful words in *East of Eden*:

> When a child first catches adults out — when it first walks into his grave little head that adults do not always have divine intelligence, that their judgments are not always wise, their thinking true, their sentences just — his world falls into panic desolation. The gods are fallen and all safety gone. And there is one sure thing about the fall of gods: they do not fall a little; they crash and shatter or sink deeply into green muck. It is a tedious job to build them up again; they never quite shine. And the child's world is never quite whole again. It is an aching kind of growing.
>
> Adam found his father out ... Who knows what causes this — a look in the eye, a lie found out, a moment of hesitation? — then god comes crashing down in a child's brain.

This failing used to remain concealed, but that's no longer the case, and the expectations resting on the shoulders of young fathers are greater than ever. So great, in fact, that some men even refuse to assume the paternal role. Others, by contrast, engage with their children far more than the previous generation. And that group of active dads are the very ones who feel they are failing in their role as father. The same is also true of mothers, incidentally.

Mothers and fathers have probably never been more conscious of their parental duties than they are nowadays. From all quarters, they are bombarded with reminders of their responsibilities and, therefore, also of their risk of failing. The journalist Kaat Schaubroeck offered a razor-sharp analysis of this in her book *Een verpletterend gevoel van verantwoordelijkheid* (*A Crushing Feeling of Responsibility*). Anything that goes wrong with a baby, a toddler, a child is the parents' fault. The wrong diet, the wrong sleeping habits, the wrong this, the wrong that. Parents appear to be caught in a perpetual performance-evaluation meeting whose outcome is a foregone conclusion. *No mercy for the weak.*

What's more, that evaluation outcome is soon adopted by their own offspring. Even young children quickly realise that their father doesn't stick to his own rules ('You didn't clean your teeth last Sunday!'). Older children discover even more transgressions ('My dad goes on sex sites!'), also by their mothers ('My mum has a profile on Tinder!'). The classic illusion is punctured; the designation 'father' no longer entails an unquestioned position of authority. Every parent now has to 'prove' him- or herself — and this is precisely the best way to set someone up to fail, since any proof will be incomplete and therefore only convincing in the short term. The feeling of superiority typical of the bygone era has now turned into shame. Self-aware fathers are perfectly conscious of the fact that they do not themselves live up to the demands they make of their children. One father of two teenage daughters told me, 'If they knew how I sometimes look at their girlfriends, they'd call me a dirty old man.'

Consequently, I can describe two extreme types of modern-day fathers. There's the father who never really accepts fatherhood and gives up trying after a short time. All his attention goes on his career and his own life, and there's no room for kids. At the other extreme, we have the very mindful father, who spends a lot of time with his children, is overprotective, studies books on parenting, and wants to be involved in everything. He becomes a kind of second mother. Which is not a good idea; one mother is enough.

They're either never present, or present too much — either way, it's never far from being a caricature. What they lack, fathers are told, is firmness, the courage to say 'No' when necessary. If they *do* do that, they get it in the neck straight away ('So old-fashioned!'). These are confusing times for men. Just think about it: they have to be friend *and* father to their children, househusband *and* macho man (but only at the appropriate moment) to their wives, colleague *and* careerist at work.

The expectations we place on parents are very ambiguous. We hear increasing calls for a return to a strict approach, since 'the youth of today' have gone too far. Parents and schools accuse each other of laxity. But anyone who takes a strict approach is showered with recriminations. We no longer want the authority of the past, but we have no new authority, either.

Paternalism: the world as a kindergarten

The aim of parenting is to make itself redundant. 'Trusting and letting go' is another way of putting it. We know that we've succeeded as parents if our children are able to leave us confidently and bring up their own children in turn. Just like in a story written by an emancipated German-Jewish woman, Glückel von Hameln, in the early 18th century:

> During a storm, a nest full of young birds is threatened with flooding. Papa bird carries his children to safety, one by one. As he flies above the swirling waters with the first fledgling in his claws, he says, 'Do you see the trouble I take to keep you safe? Will you do the same for me when I am old and weak?' 'Of course I will,' answers the first fledgling. Whereupon Papa bird promptly drops him in the water with the words, 'A liar does not deserve to be saved.' He does the same with the second fledgling. When he asks the third and last fledgling the same question, he receives the answer, 'Dear Father, I cannot promise you that. But I can promise you that I will save my own children.' Papa bird carries the young fledgling to safety.

Bringing up the next generation means trusting that they will, in their own way, be there for their children. The problems arise when that trust is lacking, or when the older generation continues to cling on to power and prevent the younger generation from growing up.

We see the same process beyond the realm of the family and parenting. A certain social class feels superior to all others, and its members patronisingly take it for granted that they should make decisions about and for all other classes. Such an attitude is called 'paternalism', a term that illustrates its connection to the patriarchy. The group that feels itself to be superior — the 'paters' — sees the others as actual children who don't know what's best for them, and so they make decisions for those 'children', in the way a 'strict but fair' father would.

In 1960, Lacan wrote a critique of a similar belief, which he claimed to have recognised among the psychotherapists of the day. Initially, this conviction sounds very positive: 'What I want is the good of others.' The therapist then takes a different direction: 'What I want is the good of others in the image of my own.' And then the sting comes in the tail: 'What I want is the good of others in the image of my own, provided that the others do not deviate from it *and* it depends on me.' The patient as a disempowered infant, unable to make the right choices, is confronted with an all-powerful father-therapist who knows what's best — and imposes it.[4]

Unjustified superiority (patronising) runs through the history of the patriarchal West like a golden thread. Whoever is in power takes decisions with far-reaching consequences on behalf of certain parts of the population without consulting those groups and without having been given a mandate by them to do so. The combination of those two characteristics is what typifies paternalism.

A crude version of it is found in the form of colonialism, when the West was assured of its own superiority for centuries. We find more veiled instances of paternalism in figures we might not expect. In the same Pensée in which Pascal undermines the foundations of law and order, he also writes that it is 'necessary to deceive men for their own good'. Voltaire, a figurehead of the Enlightenment, looked down upon the common people and found it a very good thing that they had religion. 'If God did not exist, it would be necessary to invent him.' The upper classes — the nobility, philosophers, the clergy — feel intellectually and morally superior and assume that the lower classes are stupid and immoral by nature, and that they are unable even to behave themselves properly, let alone make the right decisions. In the 19th century, the division of labour was clear. 'You keep them stupid and I'll keep them poor,' said the King to the Pope. 'And obedient,' I might add to that.

The belief that the masses are stupid is still held by many highly educated people today, and is used, among other things, as an argument against democracy. This belief is not only indicative of a misplaced sense of superiority, but also based on reasoning that's extremely dangerous since it prepares the ground for a government of 'experts', which is only a small step away from a totalitarian regime. Paternalism is not a necessity born out of the innate intellectual and moral weakness of large groups of people. On the contrary, it is the system that makes the people this way. 'What a load of lies they had us all believe!'

Paternalism finds it necessary to take decisions out of peoples' hands, and pretends while doing so that it only wants what's best for them. The former is pure abuse of power and the latter, albeit possibly well-meant, is infuriatingly patronising. It puts me in mind of a care worker in an old people's home, breezing into the room to ask, 'And how are we today?' The healthcare industry and politics are the last bastions of paternalism. But even there, the emperor is naked and his crown is increasingly slipping.

Politics as an impossible profession: 'Who believes those people anymore?'

By way of an introduction, a little romantic reading on the subject of the fatherland and politics. Imagine a country slips into a period of decline, when moral turpitude goes hand in hand with a loss of economic and political power. Unemployment is high, young people lack direction, insecurity increases, and there's often also a threat from a hostile foreign power. At that moment, a strong figure arises, a father of the fatherland, who takes the helm with a steady hand and restores norms and values. Great Britain has Churchill, France has De Gaulle. And Germany has Hitler, Iran has Khomeini, Russia has Putin …

Enlightened dictatorship is an illusion, and romance without intelligence leads directly to fascism. As an illusion, it's connected to what Freud described as the 'neurotic's family romance', namely the desire for a 'strict but fair' father. The political system has for years lived off that desire. Government leaders have portrayed themselves as good family fathers, thus reducing their voters to the position of disempowered children. Countries have invariably been referred to as the fatherland, for which every son must be prepared to sacrifice his life if necessary. Patriotism is the nephew of the patriarchy.

When World War I broke out, thousands of young men joined up voluntarily to fight. *Dulce et decorum est pro patria mori*, it is a sweet and glorious thing to die for one's country, according to the verses of Horace. And in this way an entire generation marched towards its death. How many people would volunteer today, a hundred years later? Western armies are professionalised forces, while men who fight for their God and country are called terrorists or madmen.

World War I contributed greatly to the undermining of the romantic idea of the fatherland and the political patriarchy. The ineptitude of the military and political leaders on both sides was so enormous that news of it reached the public despite censorship and unreliable reporting. Certainly, some members of the intelligentsia thought the game was up. Even just the title of Robert Graves' autobiographical account of the war years leaves nothing to the imagination: *Good-Bye to All That*. Graves was a comrade in arms of Wilfred Owen, one of the so-called War Poets: British officers who set their experiences at the front down in poetic form. Following an unbearably realistic description of a soldier's death by poison gas ('And watch the white eyes writhing in his face, / His hanging face, like a devil's sick of sin'), Owen concludes:

> My friend, you would not tell with such high zest
> To children ardent for some desperate glory,
> The old Lie: Dulce et decorum est
> Pro patria mori.[5]

Owen died exactly one week before the signing of the Armistice on 11 November 1918.

One of the ways we can view the 20th century is as the century when the political system outlived itself. Whether it was under communism, socialism, or so-called democratic centralism, the system always had the same structure. A small group of men, often led by one head honcho, took decisions for the rest of the population in the full belief that they had right on their side.[5]

A hundred years after the fiasco of World War I, belief in a father of the fatherland has almost completely disappeared — the figure has become suspect by definition. Mainstream movies are a convenient mirror of this reversal. Until about half a century ago, the following politically correct scenario appeared systematically on the silver screen: non-Western regimes (communist, African, Asian, or South American) were corrupt to the core, and run by fat, indolent dictators (who also abused the heroine). Luckily, they were challenged by the right-minded leaders of Western democracies (in the final scene, the heroine fell into the arms of her liberator). Nowadays, you can't see a political film or series about our own politicians that doesn't depict them as riddled with corruption and self-interest, from *All the President's Men* to *Borgen* and *House of Cards*. 'Politicians are all just out to line their own pockets, I tell you!'

The reality is, I think, much worse. It's not that our politicians are corrupt — although a minority certainly are — but rather that they are powerless. Our system of government is a 19th-century one, no longer suited to our modern reality, with a globalised economy and a highly educated population. 'Who believes those people anymore?' asked the Belgian leader of the opposition — a question that would be turned on him and his party as soon as they took over the running of the country.

Administrators who aim to disguise the paternalistic nature of this model are doing nothing to improve the credibility of politics and politicians. Take the following passage from the Dutch King's Speech from the Throne in 2013:

> It is an unmistakable fact that people in today's networked, information-driven society have more power over their own lives and are more independent than they were in the past. This fact, combined with the necessity to reduce the government deficit, means the classic welfare state is slowly but surely shifting towards a participation society. Anyone who can is called upon to take responsibility for his or her own life and environment.

This passage can be traced directly to a consultation document from the Dutch Council for Public Administration, entitled 'Trusting and Letting Go'. The undertone is pretty patronising: politics is done by people who stand above the citizens, who are, in fact, still children. Once those citizens show they are sufficiently adult, the patriarchal government can trust and let go of them.

What the government fails to realise is that the citizens have long-since lost any trust they had in those who govern them. '*Dis*trusting and Letting Go' would seem a more appropriate slogan here. Terms like 'trusting and letting go' and 'participation society' make it appear as if politicians want to give citizens more autonomy, but everyone knows that these are euphemisms employed to conceal swingeing cuts, and that there can be little talk of 'letting go'. Citizens are given the 'freedom' to assume certain responsibilities for themselves, within narrow, government-imposed limits, and even have the privilege of footing the bill to boot.

'Take responsibility and make your own agreements' is what this really means. The latter term is used in the same ambiguous way in education. Think of a conversation between a school teacher and her student: 'We agree that you will ...' The odd switch from the first person plural to the second person singular, from 'we' to 'you', reveals the underlying message. 'I want you to do this. If you don't do it, you will be punished.' This has little to do with a real agreement, in which both sides have a say and reach a settlement. And the situation becomes even more ridiculous if we look at what happens next. Students, or citizens, who choose not to accept the agreement are told they 'have not kept their part of the bargain'. Which brings me to the next political buzzword I've heard, 'self-responsibility', which is the just the latest way to saddle people with a sense of guilt. 'Have you really taken responsibility for yourself?'

This definition of the term 'responsibility' turns its meaning completely on its head. Legally speaking, a person can only be held responsible for something for which they are to blame. A bank and its management can be held responsible if it is revealed that they have squandered their customers' money through fraudulent activities. Shifting responsibility to the general population for the use of 12 per cent of the country's gross domestic product (GDP) to 'rescue' the banks is topsy-turvy, shifting the blame, and the debt, onto the victims.[6]

Criticism of this use of language and its implications hasn't only come from the political left. In late 2012, the Netherlands Institute for Social Research concluded: 'In many cases, more self-responsibility means that the government forces citizens to act in a way that it thinks is best.'[7] In practice, 'trusting and letting go' means passing responsibilities down to lower levels without the associated right to make decisions, *and* with a significant reduction in financial resources. Local governments are currently having to take over many responsibilities, even as their subsidies dwindle. The consequences of this aren't difficult to foresee. A large number of public services that used to be paid for collectively have now been farmed out to the private sector, with the result that less affluent citizens fall by the wayside.

The Flemish coalition-government agreement of

2014 also aims to place responsibility on citizens and give them a say. 'Trust, Connect, and Progress' is the title of the agreement. Ludo Couvreur, a Belgian biochemist and former company executive, totted up the key words in the text: 6 occurrences of 'self-reliance', 43 of 'trust', 22 of 'simplify', 2 of 'maximise', 25 of 'responsibility', 42 of 'participation', 2 of 'increasing a sense of responsibility', and 50 of 'growth'. Logic would dictate that funding should be made available for the transferral of responsibility onto the citizen. But there's no mention of such funding in the coalition agreement …

The traditional political system, on both the left and the right wings, puts me in mind of Mr Valdemar in the eponymous story by Edgar Allan Poe. Mr Valdemar is dead, but doesn't realise it. He should see a psychotherapist.

The success story of psychotherapy

The profession of the psychotherapist is a very recent one within the healthcare sector. We have Freud to thank for the term, which is barely a hundred years old. Until about halfway through the last century, Freudian psychoanalysis was the dominant form of treatment, albeit for a select group of patients only. The big breakthrough for psychotherapy came in the 1960s, when a great variety of psychotherapeutic methods were put on offer, working alongside, intertwined with, and (most often) pushing against each other. If all those different therapists had anything in common, it was their opposition to bourgeois society — as part of which they also included psychoanalysis, incidentally. Their aim was to liberate their patients from patronising structures, including the healthcare system. Ironically, one of Freud's central theses was that Victorian society was unhealthy and lay at the root of many of the neuroses of his time.

What's more, the entire healthcare sector in which psychotherapy was embedded was pervaded by a religious paternalism. Originally, almost all healthcare workers were nuns or clergymen who helped specific groups of the needy from within their congregation, ranging from children and the elderly to the physically and mentally ill, who were afforded absolutely no right to decide their own fate. It was in this patronising context that the first psychiatric treatment centres arose. Suddenly, Mother Superior had to work alongside long-haired, baggy-jumpered therapists — strange bedfellows, indeed!

The liberation psychotherapists of the '60s abandoned Freud. They sought to free the sheep, both from the flock and from the shepherd, with the alienating society being the flock, and the shepherd being the patriarch in whose name everything happened. That put psychotherapists in direct confrontation with the prevailing view within the health sector itself, which was basically designed to maintain the status quo as far as possible. The uneasy relationship between these two camps was brought most sharply into relief by the so-called anti-psychiatry movement, when individual psychiatrists challenged the system in which they were forced to work, in the belief that it was this very system that lay at the basis of many of the mental problems they had to treat.

Half a century later, psychiatry purports to be a brain science, and psychotherapy has become a respectable part of the healthcare sector. Seen from a distance, this is no doubt a success story. The amateurism of the early years has been replaced by an 'evidence-based approach' — a term commonly used in academic research to indicate that there is sound scientific proof for the efficacy of a treatment. This type of medical care, previously the preserve of the wealthier members of society, is now easily available to just about anyone, as it's subsidised by the government.

But what do we see happening? More and more, people are dropping out of the official psychotherapy circuit. The numbers of 'no shows' — the informal term for patients who fail to turn up for their appointments — are extremely high. These figures are also a source of anxiety for the therapists who work in mental-health facilities, since their funding depends on them. Moreover, it's not only the patients who are dropping out of the system; therapists also seem to have an increasingly hard time of it. Workers in the healthcare sector in general and the psychotherapy sector in particular suffer especially high rates of occupational burnout.

Clearly, something is going on. Freud called psychotherapy an impossible practice. Nowadays, therapy is extremely successful, but still its impossibility is becoming visible. Why are both therapists and patients abandoning it?

Psychotherapy often fails — and the psychotherapist along with it — because too many expectations are placed in it. As Freud wrote, we can help patients with their neurotic problems, but not with the misery of every day. Furthermore, the causes of people's problems are increasingly social in nature. Someone who's suffering mentally because they can't find a job despite constantly searching, and then also facing criticism for being a sponger, will not find an effective solution at the psychotherapist's practice. In the worst case, psychotherapy then becomes like tranquilisers prescribed for a battered wife: the pills make her numb to the abuse and she remains stuck in an extremely unhealthy situation. In both cases (existential and social problems), psychotherapists are placed in the position of the expert — thus, that of master — which is impossible to live up to. And this makes therapists sick.

So, why do patients abandon the system? I suspect that this has to do with a significant shift in the goals of psychotherapy. Some of my more cynical fellow psychotherapists say their main task these days is to work their way through waiting lists, although I wouldn't go quite that far. In the past, a psychotherapist's aim was to help people; now the implied task is to adjust them to society. For the government, psychotherapy is the new instrument of discipline. And this makes patients desert it.

The change in goal becomes particularly apparent in comparison with the early years of psychotherapy, in the 1960s and 1970s. People sought help for mental-health problems, which were generally believed to be the combined result of social (religious-patriarchal), economic (alienation at work), and individual (childhood) factors. Psychotherapy was supposed to intervene with a view to self-development and self-determination. The title of the most influential book on treatment at the time was *On Becoming a Person*, written by the founder of the 'client-centred therapy' approach, Carl Rogers. The name of this therapeutic approach, and the title of Rogers' book, speak for themselves: the focus is on the client, as a person.

Two generations later, psychologists, along with managers, have become the new guardians of order. The contrast with psychotherapy's original goal is enormous. Modern psychodiagnostics deals mostly in social standards for 'deviant behaviour'.*

The resulting therapies require people to conform to a social ideal. This ideal is currently pervaded by the doctrine of the free market. The expected norms are easy to list: assertiveness, success, flexibility, efficiency, self-confidence. In this view, problems with stress, for example, result from a false perception on the part of the patient, and not from

---

* Around the world, diagnoses of mental disorders are now based on the *Diagnostic and Statistical Manual of Mental Disorders*. In 2011, in the run-up to the release of the revised fifth edition (including more than 100 new 'disorders'), the British Psychological Society published the following criticism, among others: 'The putative diagnoses presented in DSM-V are clearly based largely on social norms, with "symptoms" that all rely on subjective judgements, with little confirmatory physical "signs" or evidence of biological causation. The criteria are not value-free, but rather reflect current normative social expectations ... We are also concerned that [diagnostic] systems such as this are based on identifying problems as located within individuals. This misses the relational context of problems and the undeniable social causation of many such problems.'

an actually stressful environment — so the patient needs to work on his or her perception.[8] Having a paid job is a must. This is paternalism rearing its head again: it's not about the wellbeing of a weaker group; it's about maintaining an established order.

This becomes clear when we consider that the United Kingdom decided in 2006 to provide substantial funding for short cognitive behavioural therapies out of labour-market concerns. That is, too many people were sitting at home with depression, which was costing industry a lot of money.[9] Of course, having a meaningful job is extremely important for our mental health. Unfortunately, for a growing group of people, today's workplace is a source of chronic stress, causing them to get sick as a result.* However, I don't think it's a good idea simply to patch

---

* Stress is a fashionable word, which means we often forget that it can be measured medically using the presence in the blood of the hormone cortisol. Heightened levels of cortisol over a protracted period of time can cause a whole range of diseases and conditions, from simple colds to cardiovascular disease, inflammation, lower-back pain, anxiety, and depression. Unfortunately, this lengthy time also makes the connection less obvious. When a miner develops silicosis or a plumber gets lead poisoning, the connection is clear. An account manager may contract an infectious disease, or develop high blood pressure, or an inflammatory disease, or depression. It's not so strange that these new occupational illnesses are seldom recognised as such. But this makes recognition all the more necessary because, today, the opposite is often the case: people who become sick due to their working conditions may be suspected of being malingerers, and then have to deal with that guilt on top of their actual sickness. (See Verhaeghe, 2013.)

them up psychologically so that they can just go back to the same work situation.

And even psychotherapists are part of the growing group of those under stress.

Carers on the couch

The decision to become a psychotherapist is not one you take just like that.* You want to help people, taking a human approach ('all those pills can't be good'). You go and study clinical psychology. The first setback is your colleagues, who are not what you expected. Their use of language is far removed from anything in the real world, the professors are disappointing, and many of your fellow students drop out, disenchanted. You persevere, because the good news is that there do seem to be some very useful psychotherapeutic methods, whose effectiveness has been demonstrated convincingly by scientific research. After getting your master's degree, you go on to complete specialist training as a therapist, in which you become so familiar with the jargon that it even starts creeping onto your everyday language. That enables you finally to get that dream job, and you can start working as a psychotherapist in a mental-health centre. Your appointments diary fills up, and now you can begin actually helping real people.

Then reality bites — the problems your clients present with are much more complex than those in the textbooks.

---

* The following describes the career path in Belgium. It differs in other countries, but is no less hard.

The efficacy of everything you learned so diligently turns out to be a good bit less than you hoped.[10] The treatment time (number of sessions) per client is drastically cut by the powers that be, with the result that you can provide little lasting help. On top of this, your clients expect you to solve all their problems by waving a magic wand, and a considerable number drop out of therapy when that turns not to be the case. These are the same clients who are allowed to judge you on a regular basis. This evaluation system is known as 'routine outcome monitoring', or ROM, and it is enough to keep you awake at night.[11]

A few years down the line, you'll have ended up in one of three possible scenarios, without even noticing it yourself. In the first, you remain actively committed to your patients, which means you often clash with the regulations of the organisation you work for: you're only allocated 16 sessions to deal with a person's problems, but you've already had 19 sessions and that is not acceptable. The gap between your level of commitment and the attitude of the management — and more broadly, the increasing amount of regulation — becomes too great to bear. You suffer burnout and have to see a therapist yourself. The second possible scenario is that you escape from the actual work you trained for by working your way up the hierarchy. You barely ever see patients anymore, so you are no longer confronted directly with the failure of their therapies. As an added extra, you also get to rap your colleagues on the knuckles when their ROM figures aren't good enough. The third scenario is that you descend into cynicism and become one of those therapists who see patients as the cause of their own problems. 'They have too little "resilience"; they're too susceptible to stress.' When therapy then fails, it is the patients' own fault, for being 'resistant to treatment'.

Luckily, there's a fourth scenario: you leave such rigid organisations and seek out colleagues who have the same experience as you and want to take a different approach. Both your clinical practice and repeated conclusions reached by clinical researchers have shown you what *really* yields results: building a supportive relationship with your clients, and the extent to which they have the opportunity to take an active part in their own therapeutic treatment. In other words: the extent to which you see and treat them as adult human beings whom you are accompanying through a process of change.

FOUR
RETURN (DARTH VADER) OR CHANGE (BIG BROTHER)?

Traditional patriarchal authority has more or less disappeared, together with the voluntary submission to a number of conventions that always flowed from it. The effects of this are felt in every possible area (emergency doctors and ticket inspectors know all about it). The search for a solution is in full swing, and two radically different responses are emerging.[1]

The first is a desperate attempt to return to the authority model of the past. This is doomed to failure since the basis of that authority has disappeared. Power without authority, and therefore with forced submission, is increasing in various sectors, such as the economy, politics, education, and even healthcare. Our phobic focus on Islamic terrorism blinds us to the far greater threat from within.

The second response is one that promises a new authority. 'New' here means with a different basis and a different way of working than the patriarchal system. It may sound surprising, but I have the strong impression that this new authority will include a radical reversal. Instead of being determined by one single, lofty body, its foundation will be horizontal and group-based. Darth Vader makes way for Big Brother.

From the father of the fatherland to the (not so) perfect son-in-law

Efforts to go back to the old system are most noticeable in politics. Every political party promises change: it's only from the government that we hear there is no alternative to current policy. Today, politicians no longer look like fathers of the fatherland, resembling rather the perfect son-in-law, who later turns out to be after the family silver. Their failure is the failure of an outdated system. When policymakers continue to cling on to such a system, there is a shift from authority to power, with an emphasis on external control and force. Political leaders turn into rulers; they are no longer figures of authority. Democracy trickles away in every direction and dictatorial regulations increase — hence the frantic attempts of many politicians to justify their actions.

Such justifications can only be given by referring to an external basis, since that is how authority works. The church, as the most important pillar of the patriarchy, has become obsolete, and now realises this itself. In late 2014, the Belgian bishops appealed for experts to assist them in dealing with paedophile priests. 'Without this support, the church authorities are scarcely able to take any decisions,' said the Bishop of Antwerp, Johan Bonny. Nationalism, too, with its references to tradition and national character, is no longer convincing, even when it's peppered with Latin phrases (*Absit invidia verbo*). The main thing is that a new basis for authority must not be open to debate, and must make people feel as secure as possible.

Politicians have now found a new basis for their authority: numbers! In the current system, any exercising of power must be accompanied by a reference to statistical material, and the ideal son-in-law turns out to be an accountant. A grudging public is overwhelmed by statistics, proving that the proposed decision is the only one possible. The majority of policy meetings start with spreadsheets, and they are indeed very hard to argue with. Numbers reflect a cool, objective reality, and are biased neither towards the political right or the left, since they are based on scientific research — at least, that's the message we're given.

Before I examine spreadsheets as the new foundation for authority, I want first to pay attention to a dual shift that takes place almost unnoticed whenever authority seeks its basis in statistics. The first concerns authority figures: who is to be the incarnation of this new authority? The second shift is even more important, and concerns the moral character of authority per se: what norms and values are contained in the numbers?

Gas chambers, gulags, and soup kitchens

The first shift is the easiest to identify. Traditional authority involves a clear chain of command, in which the highest authority figure bears the most responsibility. Each link in the chain is a representative of patriarchal authority and is in principle answerable to those above. The fact that things occasionally go dreadfully wrong with that authority doesn't detract from the clearly identifiable nature of the authority figures. In such a system, opposition can always be directed against someone who's known to have authority (the headmaster, the chief medical officer, the university chancellor, the bishop).

As soon as authority becomes based on statistics, this opportunity for targeted opposition disappears. Statistics appear to lead a life of their own within digital arteries, based on indisputable algorithms. Every so often, they leave their underground existence and surface on the screen. This appearance causes either enthusiasm or dismay among spectators, who, in either case, are spectators above all else. There's little they can do; the measures to be taken are already fixed in the figures. Thinking outside this box is impossible. You can't enter into a dialogue with numbers, and you can't just dismiss them. Responding with different figures means still thinking within the same box. Authority is no longer embodied in a person, but becomes both anonymous and autonomous. This is — as we so often hear these days — just 'the system'. And we must all defer to it.

This first shift, from a clear authority figure to an anonymous spreadsheet, makes possible the second shift, from a morally and ideologically based authority to a supposedly objective one, *and* obscures it at the same time. The most successful ideology is that which knows how to make itself invisible, and which can present its ideological character as an allegedly objective view of 'reality'.

Those who fall into this trap overlook a crucial fact. Authority is *always* based on moral assertions about the acceptable relations between parents and children, between men and women, between equals and non-equals. These relations are full of norms and values, and therefore can't be justified by objective science. A shift from a traditional to an instrumental authority based on supposedly scientific insights is downright dangerous. Both German Nazism and Russian communism proved that in the last century. In both cases, the experiment rapidly degenerated into a totalitarian regime based on an instrumental rationality in which humans were considered to be nothing more than statistics.

Now a similar, and even more dangerous, shift is taking place, yet we hardly realise it. The danger is even greater than before because the numbers are now set within a digital system of bureaucracy. Everyone has had or will have this commonplace experience at some time: an enquiry lodged with an official body doesn't elicit a particular answer (an answer that should be obvious) simply because the digital system isn't set up to deal with such a request. A less banal example is the turning back of refugees 'because the quotas have been reached'. The ultimate example is the replacement of democratic governance by financial centres that enforce decisions autonomously and anonymously, based on 'figures', once again reducing real, flesh-and-blood people to mere statistics ('the' asylum seeker, 'the' unemployed 50-year-old, 'the' single mother, 'the' entrepreneur). Weber's iron cage of bureaucracy has become a digital straightjacket, and its impersonal and even inhuman character has grown exponentially. *Computer says no.*

Statistics may well seem to provide an objective basis for authority, but they don't. Authority is always linked to human moral issues, just as the human sciences generally are — that's why they are called the humanities. The statistics used in human sciences are the result of previous choices: choices about what to 'measure', and how. Different interpretations of the questions lead to different statistics and result in different 'objective' decisions.[2]

A couple of examples can help to illustrate the link between authority, the human sciences, and moral questions. How do we study the development of a child? According to what ideal? Not so long ago, modesty was a virtue, and children were upbraided for showing off. How should we organise education? What kind of adults do we want to produce? Not so long ago, the aim was to produce critical citizens; now, the most important skill for new graduates is to be able to 'run themselves like a business', and be ready to join the labour market immediately. On what should we base our judgement of psychological normality and abnormality; should we use socioeconomic criteria, or judge by a person's own sense of wellbeing?

Which economic system should we choose (economics is not an exact science[*])? One that focuses on growth, or

---

[*] Not even for Friedrich von Hayek, one of the founding fathers of neoliberalism. When he received the Nobel Prize for Economics, he dedicated his entire prize lecture to this issue (von Hayek, 1974). The opening paragraph is striking. Speaking as an economist

rather on sustainability? How should we calculate profit and loss? Should we include environmental damage in our balance sheets? Or the increase in the number of cancer cases caused by pollution? Or the rise in public spending (our tax money) on infrastructure projects? Or should we only take into account the profits made by companies and investors?

Different questions result in different figures and therefore in different policies, which are based on differing views of people and society. Scientific methods in the human sciences can be objective, but the same isn't true of the design of the research itself. The questions used as the basis for a research project imply prior moral choices. Always, without exception. The way a question is formulated pushes our thinking in the direction of the answer. The rabbit only comes out of the hat because we put it in the hat beforehand. We lose sight of this as we are blinded by our fixation with supposedly 'objective' numbers.

Furthermore, statistics can also be used to lie very convincingly. In the hope of cutting spending on sickness

---

and, at the same time, acknowledging his own guilt, he says, 'as a profession we have made a mess of things'. For this, he blames 'the pretence of knowledge', and that also serves as the title of his address. 'It seems to me that this failure of the economists to guide policy more successfully is closely connected with their propensity to imitate as closely as possible the procedures of the brilliantly successful physical sciences — an attempt which in our field may lead to outright error.' Forty years later, Ha-Joon Chang, professor of economics at Cambridge University, said exactly the same thing — and much more — in his 2014 book, *Economics: the user's guide*.

benefits for sufferers of depression, the British government invested a very large amount of money in short-term cognitive behavioural therapy. The jubilant official and scientific evaluation came in 2008: four out of ten patients were cured! Until Paul Moloney, a practising clinical psychologist and university lecturer in Birmingham, examined the figures more closely. Half of the original group of patients dropped out of the project after (in some cases even before) the first session. Only half the patients in the remaining group completed the full course of treatment. And treatment was deemed to have been successful for one-third of those remaining patients. So, just to do the maths again: one-third of one-half of one-half: that works out at not even a 9 per cent success rate for the treatment. So where does the conclusion *four out of ten patients were cured* come from? The number is based on the people who completed the full course of treatment. The real conclusion should be: this program cost a fortune and the results are comparatively negligible.³ A more general conclusion is that it's better not to believe statistics quoted by policymakers unless you know their calculation methods.

The use of numbers, even if they are correct, clouds our awareness of the questions to which those numbers form the answers.⁴ In his humorous science-fiction series *The Hitchhiker's Guide to the Galaxy*, Douglas Adams describes Deep Thought, a computer designed specially to give the answer to the ultimate question of Life, the Universe, and Everything. After 7.5 million years of calculations, Deep Thought comes up with the answer: 42. When asked for further explanation, the computer points out that the answer seems incomprehensible because the questioners never really understood what the real question was. To find that out would require the construction of an even more powerful computer.[5]

The debate should not be about numbers per se, but about the design of studies and the conceptual framework that produce those figures. The likelihood that such a debate will take place is extremely small, precisely because of the failure to recognise that 'the figures' are based on moral positions. Anyone who tries to launch such a debate, for example concerning a plan to slash university funding mostly by cutting lecturers' positions, will soon be told they are 'not being realistic' and that they 'need to keep both feet on the ground'. This gives the impression that figures are a reflection of 'reality'.

Acolytes of this cult of numbers are indeed convinced that they're able to see 'reality' (by which I mean the reality of our society) 'as it really is', in contrast to previous generations whose view of 'reality' was entirely coloured by ideology. The acolytes have freed themselves of this; they see things truly, and anyone who comes after them will be unable to improve on their ideas very much at all.

Such arrogance is timeless, and its clearest expression can be found in the work of the German philosopher Hegel. He believed he could identify an inexorable process of evolution through history, with an inescapable internal logic, moving towards a glorious climax. For Hegel, that climax came at the beginning of the 19th century, after which everything would remain pretty much the same.

More recently, we find the same view in the work of Francis Fukuyama, who, in 1992, also proclaimed the end of history, after which we would all enter a post-ideological paradise (Fukuyama has since changed his mind).

The Nazis predicted the thousand-year Reich of the Aryan race, communists looked forward to a timeless proletarian paradise, and both were convinced that they were the culmination of the evolutionary process. In turn, the doctrine of the free market assumes that its vision is the only accurate representation of 'reality' ('there is no alternative') and that its universal implementation will eventually lead to an entrepreneurial paradise with prosperity (and democracy) for all.

Marxism was at least sufficiently in touch with reality to acknowledge the price tag for a proletarian paradise, which would only come after a period of 'creative destruction'. Marxism certainly kept that part of its promise. The same expression — creative destruction — was adopted by neoliberalists, and their promise now appears to be coming true, too.

Nazism led to the gas chambers, communism led to the gulags, and neoliberalism leads to soup kitchens.

Pseudo-authority based on pseudo-exactitude

The human sciences aren't exact, and adapting methods from the exact sciences to such disciplines as psychology, social studies, and economics has largely proven to be a failure. Economics provides the starkest example of this, and has recently been described as 'the only academic discipline that derives its existence from retrospectively explaining why it was previously wrong'.[6]

Mathematics is one of the greatest inventions of the human mind, and it's no coincidence that the oldest-known writing system was principally used to record numbers at first. The precision of mathematics opens up enormous possibilities, including the capacity of numbers to allow us to generalise. Ten is ten, always and everywhere, and the difference between ten and eight is always precisely two, just like the difference between 1399 and 1401. This precision means we can carry out mathematical operations, from simple counting and multiplication, all the way to computerised formulae — and the results always come out exactly the same.

The number of practical applications of mathematics is now literally astronomical. After a journey of ten years, five months, and four days, which took it around the Sun five times on a little jaunt of no less than 6.5 billion kilometres, the Rosetta spacecraft finally arrived at its destination: the comet 67P. Both the comet's orbit and the trajectory of the space probe were calculated years earlier. This is mathematics at its best.

However, ten is not ten everywhere, and the difference between six and eight is not always precisely two. What I'm talking about are measurements in the human sciences. Here's an example of what I mean.

> Please tick the statement that corresponds best
> to your level of agreement with the statement
> 'I am willing to tolerate stinging nettles on the

roadside to give rare butterfly species a chance
of survival'.

(5) strongly agree

(4) agree

(3) neither agree nor disagree

(2) disagree

(1) strongly disagree

Familiar? Undoubtedly. We're dished up questions like this regularly, concerning all sorts of issues, sometimes with different wording, but always asking about a little bit more or a little bit less agreement. Then you sit and ponder awhile whether you 'agree' or 'strongly agree'. But, after a while, you fill it out quickly to get it over with. Such questionnaires are based on a method that's used frequently in the human sciences, the so-called Likert scale. It yields numerical results, and therefore creates the impression that it is a 'measurement', in which different numbers (you tick 5, I tick 4) and the same numbers (we both tick 5) can occur.

These are not actual numbers (such as those that mathematicians call 'natural' numbers); rather, they indicate a difference (an 'interval') between some amount and a little bit more. Between natural numbers, two and three, for example, or four and five, the difference is always the same; in this case, one. But the difference between (2) 'disagree' and (3) 'neither agree nor disagree' on the one hand, and (5) 'strongly agree' and (4) 'agree' on the other, is not necessarily the same, and even less so when the evaluation comes from different people. These differences (which statisticians call 'interval measurements') can be sometimes larger, sometimes smaller; we can literally only guess. The same is true of the significance of numbers that look the same: does the 4 I tick enthusiastically mean the same as the 4 the lady next-door ticks hesitantly?

In other words, this kind of measurement never results in precise numbers. This fact is 'forgotten' in a lot of research; the responses of the people surveyed are collated and then these unreal numbers are used as the basis for statistical processes. Any mathematician, any exact scientist, knows that this is nonsense.

Serious academics in the human sciences don't make this mistake. But they face a different challenge. In order to make real measurements, a precise unit is necessary, such as centimetres for length, kilograms for weight, or cubic metres for volume. There's no debate about such measures; they express real numbers, which are confirmed by each new measurement. But what's the precise unit of measurement for intelligence? 'IQ!' cries the first-year student. But then how can it be that Paul performs differently in three different IQ tests on the same day, each one indicating a different IQ, consistently on the low side, admittedly, but still considerably different? And how come every IQ test systematically delivers higher scores after a period of a few years, compared to those attained in the initial period after its introduction (the so-called Flynn effect)? Imagine measuring the size of your kitchen window using three different tools — a carpenter's rule, a tape measure, and a laser measure — and finding that each measurement yields a significantly different answer. And imagine that the same window suddenly appears to be bigger when you measure it some years later, even using the exact same well-cared-for tools.[7]

Measuring becomes even more difficult in the case of emotionally charged issues, such as happiness, racism, empathy, integration of immigrants, and so on. Nonetheless, many studies of such questions have been carried out and their results presented numerically. These numbers are then used as the basis for statistical operations that lead to 'exact' scientific conclusions. They, in turn, are used as the basis for policy decisions, which often have a considerable impact on the lives of individuals. Everything is presented as supported by objective science and therefore not up for discussion. The numbers 'are what they are', and there is no need to think any further.

Or is there? When you look at several studies from the same field on the same subject, you'll often see widely differing results. Even non-specialists realise this, since clashes between academics are now played out in the media, even clashes over the use of statistics.

Towards the end of his career, Roger Standaert, a Belgian educationalist and researcher, published a book called *De becijferde school* (*The Quantified School*), a critical and, to my mind, nuanced discussion of the use and abuse of scientific figures in education policy. I was one of the introductory speakers at the launch of his book. Among other things, I spoke about how science is rapidly losing its position of authority, precisely because human scientists constantly contradict each other, each wielding their own set of numbers, which the newspapers make convenient use of by fishing for editorial pieces by 'authoritative scientists' eager to disprove each other's research results. In the week that followed its launch, Standaert's book prompted almost-daily scientific opinion pieces in the newspaper *De Standaard*, each contradicting the one from the day before, only to be refuted in turn by the next day's piece ... with the result that no one had any more faith in (this kind of) science; it's just one opinion after another.

This lack of faith in 'the' numbers means that science is losing its authority. And the shift towards power is one step closer.

Over-regulation as a failure of authority

Authority functions on the basis of an internalised norm, from whence comes the voluntary submission it requires. Whenever a group shares the same authority, there is great shared trust (everyone follows the same social codex, even though it's almost never written down). When authority falls away, the result is a general mistrust and a self-replicating virus of regulatory measures. Power functions by means of external control and coercion, but this inevitably provokes resistance and rebellion. Each confrontation with power lays the foundation for the next, creating a vicious circle. Control mechanisms and coercive measures become increasingly widespread, with the ultimate aim of total control.

However, the result is precisely the opposite. Attempting to render everything controllable results in nothing working as it should. Any teacher will tell you: the more rules and control mechanisms a school introduces, the less authority there is in the classroom. The result: teachers barely get a chance to do any teaching; all their attention is taken up by making sure all those regulations are being enforced and observed.

One of the most palpable consequences of the disappearance of authority is regulatory diarrhoea. Those who blame this exclusively on 'the government' (and therefore argue for its abolition) forget that we see the most important illustration of this phenomenon in the banking sector. Lack of authority leads to a flood of rules and control systems, which in turn form the basis for yet more new rules. It has reached a point where we are all sinking into a Kafkaesque quagmire. These days, a contract is necessary for just about anything, and if not a contract, then at least there must be a 'protocol', a detailed set of guidelines for procedures that must be followed in given circumstances. The aim of such regulations isn't to increase quality. Control is used because there's no trust of others, it's a protection against any possible complaints, and it provides an ability to apportion blame when things go wrong.

The roots of this lie in American management practice, which traditionally works according to a command-and-control system where everything must be decided and directed centrally. Thanks to multinational corporations and the doctrine of the free market, this has also become widespread in Western Europe. Furthermore, the marketisation of everything — government, education, research, healthcare — has created a hyper-competitive 'struggle for life', creating more mistrust. In recent years, even the education system has fallen prey to this development. Parents have realised that enrolling their children in school amounts to signing a contract. And if Junior fails to do well, it's perfectly possible to challenge the contract legally. Before you know it, every school needs a lawyer on its payroll.

Such over-regulation is doomed to fail for the same reasons that traditional authority is vanishing: the external guarantee is gone; there can be no more talk of 'voluntary submission'. The increasing number of rules, which are the typical result of the disappearance of authority, can then only work on the basis of power and enforced submission. Soon, this develops into a spiral: enforcement sparks resistance and rebellion, leading to yet more rules, yet more control of their observance, and yet more measurements — until it reaches a pathological level.[8]

Top-down versus bottom-up

Our era faces a huge challenge: how can we introduce the authority we so bitterly need without relapsing into the paternalistic model or surrendering ourselves to a dictatorship of numbers?

I agonised long over this question, but to no avail, because I was constantly searching for something that (I did not realise at the time) was also part of the classic model of authority. Every incarnation of patriarchal, and therefore also pyramidal, authority has its own, all-encompassing story, a 'narrative' (from the Bible to Mao's Little Red Book). Therefore, I thought, any new authority can only establish itself if everyone shares a new 'great story'. But where are we to find such a story, and how are we to share it?

Finally, I realised that these 'great stories' are primarily intended to keep the lowest levels of the pyramid compliant. They are part of a strategy first formulated by Plato: keep the people obedient and faithful, delude them with images of a paradise in the hereafter (or eternal punishment), and place this in the context of a great and, most importantly, compelling story. A new Bible will not provide the solution, but would merely be a new variation on what we've already had.

Sometimes, the answer is so obvious that we fail to see it when it's right under our nose. In this case, the answer is in the question. What other source of authority can we find that would be shared by a large group of people? The answer is: the group itself can function as the basis for authority — the group as a mostly horizontally functioning network that confers constantly shifting authority on various figures.

Darth Vader and Big Brother

Darth Vader is a character from the *Star Wars* film series. He's the dangerous, evil leader who renounced his original ideals and went over to the 'Dark Side'. The fact that later in the series he turns out to be the father of the virtuous main character, Luke Skywalker, is a pithy reversal of the classic story of the primal father. In the *Star Wars* version, the father is evil and the son is good, and the son must defeat the father, after which it turns out that Luke's dead father had returned to the Light. The Christian church fathers would have had quite a problem with this apocryphal reading of the Redeemer.

Such father-son relationships now belong to the world of fantasy. The real world we live in is ruled by Big Brother. The mention of this name will put many readers in mind of the eponymous reality-television show, in which people (locked up in a shared house) were constantly filmed and in turns had to make confession to Big Brother, an unseen figure who (together with the television viewers) saw everything. However, the term 'Big Brother' was originally coined by George Orwell. In his novel *1984*, he envisioned a totalitarian society in which everyone is under constant surveillance via ubiquitous television screens, which not only broadcast images, but also record them. We're not so far removed from this scenario today. The screen I'm using to write this text has an integrated camera, as do my tablet and my smartphone.

Orwell casts a sharp light on the dangers of such total, centralised control, and of course he's absolutely right to do so. Big Brother as described by him is a technologised dictatorship, in which it has become unclear whether the great leader actually exists or not. On closer inspection, this is revealed to be a digital version of God's all-seeing and all-controlling eye. Consequently, *1984* remains an example of pyramidal authority, with no hint of horizontality at all.

My interpretation of Big Brother is radically different and is more closely related to the social control exercised by people among themselves. The village communities of the past are a good illustration of this. Everybody knew everybody else's business, and so everybody was forced to adhere to the collective rules. Horizontally exercised authority such as this is extremely coercive — the sanction is exclusion from the group — and can take on particularly cruel forms. Those who claim that horizontal social control is inherently good, and vertical, patriarchal authority is by definition bad, are deluding themselves.

The reason I highlight the horizontal authority of Big Brother is not because I believe it's always the better option, but because I am in no doubt that this is becoming the new reality, partly due to digitisation, but also partly due to the higher level of education among the general population. When Kant made his plea for us to liberate ourselves from nonage in 1784, 80 per cent of his compatriots were illiterate, and printed books had only become common a century before. The fact that society at the time was ruled in a pyramidal way, with a 'father of the fatherland' at the top, was not so strange at the time. This is no longer the case.

The fundamental change that has taken place is evidenced by modern education as the natural model for authority. Under the old model, a child came into contact with only a very limited number of people, who were part of a clear hierarchy, with the father at the top, followed by teachers, priests, clergymen, etc. The vast majority of children's education and upbringing took place in the domestic environment because that's where children spent most of their time.

The situation today is completely different. My granddaughter, born as she was into a more-than-privileged environment, constantly leaves her purely domestic environment at the age of just six months. Luce spends three days a week at a creche, one day a week with one of her grandmas, and one day with the other, and always from early in the morning. She comes home at just about bedtime. Her parents see their child two days a week. So who is raising her? What's more, the number of people responsible for her upbringing and education, as well as the places she frequents, will only increase in the future. The outside world is no longer the outside world: it's just the world. And it will not be long before the virtual world, via various screens, begins to play a prominent part in her little world.

Where and with whom do we place authority when it comes to education? As soon as a problem occurs, it becomes evident how much debate this question triggers. The school places responsibility on the child's parents, and the parents place responsibility on the school; the grandparents criticise their children for being too lenient or too strict with their grandchildren, and so on. This game of ping-pong is still centred on a search for someone who is 'the' authority, while ignoring a fact that's now become a reality: authority is shared by a group. Just like the patriarchy, the nuclear family has become a thing of the past; our children are raised by a number of people, a collective. The question is how we can develop that collective into a conscious authority.

Big Brother takes over

Authority works on the basis of voluntary submission, but that doesn't come from nowhere. Children will only submit in this way if they're exposed to an external coercive force that's of long-enough duration. Sometimes this coercive force remains in place for too long: a paternalistic government continues to treat adult citizens like children. Until about halfway through the last century, many Flemish households still had on their wall at home a picture of an eye looking straight out into the living room, with the inscription: 'God is watching you. No swearing here.' The generation I belong to were made to learn the catechism by heart, which began with the question: 'Where is God?' Answer: 'God is everywhere, in heaven above and on the Earth below, and in every place.' Next question: 'Does God see and know all things?' Answer: 'God sees all things, even our most secret thoughts. He knows all things, even those that are yet to come.'

The message was clear: there's no escaping this controlling eye. In 1791, Jeremy Bentham, a British legal philosopher, used this principle in the design of his Panopticon (literally: all-seeing). Bentham's plan was for a circular structure with a central tower surrounded by cells whose windows look out onto the interior of the building. One overseer in the tower is sufficient to control all the cells. The classic application of the Panopticon principle is in prisons or psychiatric buildings, but it can also be used for factories or office complexes. It's not difficult to imagine the Panopticon as an architectural representation of traditional authority. 'The people' are literally and figuratively looked down upon. The controlling eye is always accusing, and sees even your most secret thoughts (although the eye itself is invisible). This explains why a patriarchal culture is a breeding ground for guilt and neuroses.

A different kind of authority presupposes a different kind of Panopticon. The observation chamber at the top of the tower is no longer manned. It has been replaced by a powerful computer server that enables anybody to monitor anybody else. We live in the age of Big Brother, in which we constantly reveal ourselves (some of us quite literally) to anyone who wants to look. The net result of this is increasing horizontal control of everyone by everyone else, in contrast to the patronising vertical gaze of one guard.

This control takes place via so-called social media — Facebook, Twitter, Instagram, LinkedIn, blogs, and so on. Famous people have to become even more famous by 'telling all' about themselves in specially designed formats on TV and the radio. Unknown people hope to become famous by doing the same thing, with the result that the intimacy of the confessional or consultation room is splashed across the big screen for all to see. We no longer hide ourselves from view; on the contrary, postmodern people deliberately put themselves on show, with all that that entails. Thus, they submit voluntarily to the controlling gaze of others, and even become depressed when too few people show an interest ('How many Facebook friends do you have?'). Polish sociologist Zygmunt Bauman devised a very fitting term for this: we are living in a Do-It-Yourself Panopticon.[9]

There's a colossal difference between this and the patriarchal model. During the patriarchy, we identified ourselves through the commands and prohibitions of the father figure, out of a fear of punishment or damnation. Now, we identify ourselves through the 'likes' we receive from others (our mirror images), out of a fear of exclusion. The pressure generated by social control is huge and requires everyone to engage in a new kind of voluntary submission. If we fail, we feel ashamed and depressed. Depression has now replaced neurosis.

The possibility of escaping this is smaller than ever. The patriarchal system still maintained certain illusions. We could escape to another place (where we would run into a different version of the father). Now, there is no 'other place'; the world is full. Or, we could kill the prevailing father figure and replace him with a better one (who would not turn out to be much better in retrospect). But Big Brother cannot be killed, since he is virtual and nameless, a ghost mouse-clicking his way around the World Wide Web. The controlling gaze of everyone over everyone else is a virtual reality, and not only because of increased camera surveillance. We choose it for ourselves.

Reactions to the phenomenon of social media are predominantly negative. Conservatives deplore the disappearance of traditional norms and values, liberals mourn the loss of individual liberties, and both decry the end of privacy. Most intellectuals point to the excesses of social media: abuse by 'ordinary' people (hate campaigns, cyberbullying), by the government (social control), and by the market (targeted advertising).

In short, both the left and the right deplore the disappearance of a top-down authority, which, for me, is just one more illustration of how rapidly we forget things. In its religious, political, and pedagogical versions, the patriarchal system was a disaster for at least half of humanity (women), but, in fact, it was disastrous for just about everyone. Without being blind to the excesses of Big Brother, we must ask ourselves the following question: would we rather choose a top-down authority based on an imposed narrative, or a horizontal authority based on mutual social control? Although, in fact, reality has already chosen for us, and our options revolve mainly around how we are going to deal with this choice.

Two currently rather isolated voices make a clear choice in favour of horizontally operating social control: the elderly French philosopher Michel Serres and the Italian writer Alessandro Baricco have very optimistic ideas about digital evolution.[10] In his book *Thumbelina*, Serres subtly points out that in the pre-digital age, hundreds of millions of people died in the name of central authority (*Dulce et decorum est pro patria mori*). He believes the disappearance of a top-down society, together with the end of stable-but-rigid groups, is a great thing. For him, the rise of 'connected collectives' — groups that may be interlinked but retain their individuality — can be nothing other than progress. The earlier complicity of the patriarchy (disguised as loyalty) must make way for transparency, and obligation must make way for accountability.

In his book *The Barbarians*, Baricco pulls off a masterstroke. Initially, intellectual readers think they've found a likeminded ally in their opinions about the populist, lowbrow nature of everything to do with the internet. It's barbarian, right? By the end of the book, the same readers are convinced that the internet is quietly responsible for creating far more real democracy than they ever thought. A horizontal democracy, in stark contrast to the traditional 'democratic centralism' that the vast majority of politicians still swear by.

Both Serres and Baricco stress the fact that until very recently there was never any 'democracy of knowledge'. Knowledge was the preserve of the privileged class, who looked down upon the common people. Thanks to their knowledge, the privileged class were able to make the 'right' decisions — or so they thought. In her stark review of history, the American historian Barbara Tuchman shows the tragic injustice of many of those decisions. The title of her book speaks for itself: *The March of Folly*. Nowadays, knowledge is available to anyone, and the most important mistake politicians and leaders consistently make is to underestimate 'the common people'. The acid regurgitations of the internet (where there's no difference between knowledge, information, and publicity; people are turned into morons by the digital world; the net is seething with porn and violence; and so on) do not outweigh the fact that the internet allows anyone to search for and disseminate any knowledge. It is precisely the latter that closed communities, from incest families to dictatorships and big banks, seek to prevent at any cost.

Today's information overflow reveals the huge differences of the horizontal compared to the vertical model: there is transparency and there is no obligatory loyalty anymore. Everyone becomes increasingly visible for everyone else. There's only *one* Darth Vader, while we are *all* potential Big Brothers. Patriarchal systems rely on secret, backroom politics; Big Brother, by contrast, relies on a far-reaching openness.

Horizontal authority exercised by a group — it sounds both implausible and frightening. Since time immemorial, the tiny top layer of the pyramid has harboured a mixture of disdain for and fear of what it used to call 'the people' and now calls 'the voters'. The masses are ignorant, little more than 'electoral sheep', driven to the slaughterhouse of the voting booths every few years, right? And a group surely can't be an efficient leader, can it?

Fear of the irrational masses

Throughout the history of politics, there has always been fear of the masses, called the 'plebs' by the Senators of Rome, with images of riots, arson, and plunder. They needed to be controlled from above.

That a leaderless mob can develop a dynamic of its own, and that this dynamic can be very dangerous, was pointed out as early as the 19th century by the French social psychologist Gustave Le Bon. In his 1895 work *The Crowd: a study of the popular mind*, he examines the behaviour of the insurgent masses during the French Revolution. He concludes that people acting as a group relapse to the level of the group's stupidest member, and the crowd's basest passions rise to the top. Twenty-five years later, Freud studied organised groups with a *Führer* at their head. He, too, warned of the dangers — Freud would live just long enough to see the accuracy of his depiction confirmed by events.[11]

Both types of group will be used as an argument against horizontal authority. And both have little or nothing to do with horizontal authority as I understand it. A mob exercises power; a centrally led group is an example of top-down authority. For many people, there's absolutely no doubt that central leadership is necessary, because, in their view, a group of 'ordinary' people doesn't have the ability to make the right decisions. Listen to public opinion, they say, and then you'll see how it is.

Public opinion is crucial and can, for example, alter the electorate's voting behaviour. Politicians will do anything to win over voters, in the assumption that public opinion can be manipulated and that they are the best candidates to take control of that manipulation — spin doctors and marketing agencies are in high demand during elections. Politicians also assume that voters are basically incapable of thinking for themselves and are barely able to make decisions independently. The same assumption leads politicians to believe that government should remain in the hands of a small but highly educated elite. It should preferably be democratically elected, but when necessary (in times of crisis, for example), democratic principles can be pushed somewhat into the background. Experts will then decide what's best for 'the people'.

This view once again testifies to a paternalistic outlook, the 'father knows best' model. It fails to recognise at least three things. The small, highly educated group often takes decisions that benefit that small group, and which aren't necessarily in the interests of society as a whole. The group's level of knowledge is often far more limited than generally thought, and its actions are often revealed to be drastically mistaken in retrospect. For the past two generations, 'the people' have been far more highly educated than they ever were before. The irony of history is that this was a result of paternalism, which, in its better incarnations, supported a policy of 'betterment of the people', including, for example, making education more accessible to all. But the fathers of the fatherland must learn to let their sons (and, most importantly, their daughters) go.

That authority is best founded on knowledge is obvious, and it's also true of horizontally organised authority. As mentioned earlier, objective knowledge has no social purpose per se. In order to determine which direction we want to move in, it will be necessary to make moral choices. A group is perfectly able to acquire knowledge and to make choices in the best interests of the community, and to take a long-term view when doing so. We have seen many convincing examples of this, in both economics and politics. All that's holding us back from making the transition to this new form of government is our fear of change and our inability to break out of entrenched patterns of behaviour.

Command and control versus
Führen durch Anträge

Alongside fear of the irrational masses, there's another argument against horizontal authority, one which is of a more pragmatic nature: surely such a thing can't function without someone making the decisions and monitoring whether they're properly implemented? Ask people whether they believe decisions can be left to a group and their answers will be overwhelmingly negative. Such a thing would lead to chaos and anarchy — that is the opinion of many people.

Watch any popular film about World War II and you'll see the following scenario. On one side, you have the strictly hierarchical German army, where not a single subordinate would ever take it into his close-cropped head to contradict his superior officer. *Jawohl, Herr Leutnant!* — followed by a click of the heels. On the other side, you have the American army, with Joe and Bill chatting light-heartedly to Jack (their Captain) about tactics. Tactics that GI Joe will change at his own discretion on the battlefield if necessary, depending on what he considers best at that time. Fascism versus democracy, hierarchy versus autonomy, *Kadavergehorsamkeit* ('zombie-like obedience') versus free enterprise ... No wonder that the Germans are eventually defeated, leaving the GIs to march across Europe celebrating their victory.

Popular history is written by the victors and is always a falsification. Academic historiography paints a very different picture. German soldiers operated in autonomous units and constantly revised decisions on the battlefield about the best way to react to a situation. American soldiers executed orders that were based on detailed plans, devised and imposed by a central leadership. The result? The German soldiers inflicted twice as many casualties on the Allies as they suffered themselves, even in battles where the Germans were outnumbered and couldn't rely on support from the air force. Germany eventually lost the war due to a lack of men and resources, while the Allies could rely on a larger supply of both.

The far-reaching autonomy of the Germans on the battlefield was no accident. A hundred years earlier, Count Helmuth von Moltke, a field marshal in the Prussian army, had analysed Prussia's defeat at the hands of Napoleon. He concluded that detailed plans devised at headquarters can never respond to the reality on the ground. Today, Moltke would be an advocate of chaos theory. On the basis of his analysis, he developed his method of *Führen durch Aufträge*, leadership by means of assigning missions to subordinates, as opposed to the earlier tactic of *Führen durch Befehl*, or 'leading by command', in which specific orders were given to subordinates. In *Führen durch Aufträge*, a unit is assigned an objective, but receives no detailed plan of how to achieve it. The unit must decide on the best course of action, and is best equipped to do so, since it's the soldiers in the unit who have the best insight into the situation on the ground. This command method encourages personal initiative and responsibility as much as possible.

By the time of World War II, the Germans had developed this method even further. Forget the traditional division into artillery, tank units, and infantry (all competing with one another); forget the classic, hierarchical army structure; and rather promote a structure of cooperation, relying on soldiers' sense of responsibility and initiative. This idea gave rise to so-called *Kampfgruppen* ('combat groups'), which were ad hoc combined arms formations of various units (from regiments to platoons) and different weapons (tanks, artillery, infantry), commanded on the ground by the highest ranking officer present. They were formed and deployed to complete one specific mission.

The Allies were stumped (which division were they actually facing off against?). By the time headquarters had changed its original plans and communicated the change to the units on the ground, it was often far too late. But the Americans stuck steadfastly to their own system; each battle was meticulously prepared, planned, and executed. 'Compliance' was the key word, and millions of young American men were drilled to comply. On the other side of the frontline stood a million young German men who had been trained to make independent evaluations of a constantly changing situation and to make decisions aimed at completing the mission at hand. 'Confidence' was the key word here.[12]

Which car do you prefer to drive, an American one or a German one?

Purpose, knowledge, and the right to decide

The *Kampfgruppen* were efficient, yes, but literally deadly. Horizontal groups can also do terrible things — and this is certainly the case if they have no right to decide their own objectives. Within the pyramidal authority model of the German army, missions were imposed by a higher decision-making body; horizontal authority remained limited to the execution of the mission.

The two armies, American and German, each illustrate in a different way how pyramidal authority eventually fails. The American supreme command was highly efficient, and obstinately continued to make decisions that the people on the ground knew full well had already been rendered obsolete by events. The German high command assigned missions that not only were immoral, but also sent the combat groups to their doom. The people on the ground knew this full well, too, but they remained faithful to authority to the very end.

If we are to have horizontal authority at the level of society, then at least three conditions must be met. Knowledge must be sufficiently widespread, moral objectives must be determined by the horizontal group, and that group must function in line with self-imposed rules. The ideal combination is therefore a horizontally structured group that's mindful of the long-term goals that will benefit society; which has, or can acquire, the required knowledge to do that; and which makes, implements, or commissions the implementation of decisions to that end.

Primus inter pares

Horizontal authority is not based on the illusion that all human beings are the same. Within each group, there will be differences as well as similarities between people, and the crucial question remains how social relations should be organised.

Top-down authority has a pyramid structure in which the highest echelons are the most secure in their position, with very little movement, and what movement there is is usually only possible by toppling someone from their position. Such authority works literally in terms of commands, and the lower echelons have little or no autonomy. This system has the advantage of clarity — a classical organisational chart shows where the power rests, and will remain.

Authority that works horizontally presupposes a lot of room for movement among authority figures. There's no permanent leader, someone who occupies that position for life, so to speak, and whose person merges with the position itself. The opportunity for horizontal movement is directly contrary to that model, and a classical organisational chart is unimaginable. At first sight, such a system conjures up fears of ambiguity and lack of certainty, but that's mainly because we traditionally expect something that *can* be represented by an organisational chart. If we cast off this expectation, the advantages become obvious: more efficiency, thanks to more flexibility, and a commitment to shared goals.

It's no coincidence that voices are now being raised in the world of management to call for a change in leadership culture, away from top-down models, with the argument that new forms of leadership would be better for the organisation concerned. This is not so surprising. In a pyramidal system, the main objective of those at the top is to preserve their own position, not that of the organisation. Everything revolves around their person — and note that the system invites this. The aim of those who command authority in a horizontal system is to contribute to the organisation itself by promoting as much cooperation as possible. This means the leader can be far better described as *primus inter pares*, the first among equals. This focus on cooperation means that one of the most important tasks of leaders becomes to mediate between different members of the collective in the pursuit of a common goal. The idea that individuals must solve their own problems alone no longer exists. Authority is not seen as 'natural' due to the position a person occupies within a hierarchy, but is conferred by the fact that that person speaks for the whole group. Hence it's possible to share authority and to pass it on from one person to another, with the aim of achieving common objectives.

Mediation has become established pretty much everywhere, including in the legal system, for example. This is an important example of a social shift. While judges used to decide independently on the fates of citizens (who had no say in the matter and required an 'advocate' at court in the form of a lawyer), there is an increasing move to set up mediation bureaus. More and more people are calling on the services of mediators. The name of this profession expresses its function well: mediators do not try to impose what they think is the best decision, but help the parties involved to sort out what is acceptable to both or all of them by mutual agreement.

One difference that is characteristic of the distinction between pyramidal and horizontal authority has to do with mistakes. When authority is based on a patriarchal system, making a mistake is fatal for the alpha male. He falls (downward motion) from his pedestal, and there will already be someone ready to take his place. This leads to mistakes being concealed out of fear; in this model, the last thing a leading figure will do is to admit to a mistake. The fault always lies with somebody else.

In the horizontal authority model, anyone who errs does not tumble, since there are no higher positions. A member of the collective can make a mistake, then change his or her opinion or behaviour without being shot down for it. Often, the opposite is the case: those who admit to their mistakes and call on help from others to rectify them are seen as stronger than those who try to hide their failings.

Other people are not the enemy. Other people are very much like me and you, and we share the same goals.

INTERMEZZO

I graduated in June 1978 and started my first job one month later. I stayed in my university city, Ghent, while the vast majority of my student friends went back to where they had come from. It was to be a lonely summer: I had to go out to a public telephone box whenever I wanted to make a call. I had no television, and all my information came from just one newspaper. Personal computers did not yet exist, let alone the internet.

Thirty years later, I am giving an introductory lecture to my second-year psychology students. During the break, I receive a text from my son: 'You're talking too fast. All my mates are asking if you can slow down!!!' He's on his way back from his holidays, on the road somewhere, which in no way prevents him from being in constant contact with anyone he wants. He never reads a newspaper, but he's better informed and more critically discerning than both his parents put together. After the break, I change the speed I speak at, and that evening I receive an email from my son telling me that the second half of my lecture was much easier to follow. And, can he bring his dirty washing round the day after tomorrow?

In those 30 years, we have surfed into a new age.

The evolutionary history of our species can be divided into three periods. First, we were nomads, 'hunter-gatherers' who migrated with the seasons and food sources. There weren't many of us, but, judging by the artefacts found by archaeologists, there was a lot of exchange between different groups.

Next, we became sedentary farmers who accumulated possessions. Our settlements grew into cities, where not so long ago industry eventually developed. It was in this period that the same social structure developed all over the world, which can best be summed up as the patriarchy. It can best be imagined as a pyramid, preferably surrounded by a high wall and a deep moat.

Now we're turning into a new kind of nomad; we're all constantly on the move, even when we don't leave our homes. The sedentary-patriarchal period is coming to an end, and we're moving into the digital age. We surf around the internet, and the possibilities for interaction have increased to a dizzying degree. The vertical pyramid has had to make way for a horizontal network.

This comparison between a pyramid and a network shows how radically different our age is. A flat surface instead of depth and height, sideways movement instead of digging or climbing, connecting nodes instead of top positions, constant motion instead of standstill, open instead of closed, transparent instead of opaque.

Hannah Arendt was right when she said that (patriarchal) authority disappears when its basis collapses. What she could not have foreseen was that the cause of that collapse could be technological in nature. The digital network undoubtedly delivers the final blow to any pyramidal organisation.

Every now and then, we hear talk of the 'new humans'. But however new we are, there's at least one activity that, I suspect, occupied our hunter-gatherer forebears just as much as it does today's 'digital natives': talking about other people. Gossiping, chatting, warning, praising, criticising — all shades are possible. The effects of all this interaction are familiar to us. Those who earn a bad reputation in society may as well forget it. Those who show themselves to be trustworthy will gain the confidence of others.

No one wants to be excluded from the group; everyone has an interest in having a good standing. There are two ways we can earn a good reputation. First, by conforming as far as possible with the expectations of the group. The pressure exerted by groups, and the associated social control, is huge (just try defending an unpopular opinion against the majority view). The second way is to conceal anything we suspect might damage our reputation. Woe betide us if the community at large discovers our duplicity — we'll be tarred and feathered, and, in the worst case, the only option may be to move house.

Maintaining a spotless reputation is of life-and-death importance for anyone in a position of authority. This explains one of the typical features of the patriarchal system and pyramidal authority: the code of silence. *Omertà* or loyalty; the difference between the two is slight, and both have the same effect: social control is no longer possible.

Half a century ago, the scandal-hit director of the International Monetary Fund, French politician Dominique Strauss-Kahn, would most probably have become the president of France, despite admitting 'inappropriate' relations with a hotel chambermaid, which she alleged were attempted rape. Now, his career is irreparably ruined. In the modern world, the social control exercised by the net is the new authority, exclusion takes just one click of a computer mouse, and moving house is no longer a way to escape.

It's true that we still need to learn how to deal with this new situation. We may be digital natives, but 'digital infants' might be a more accurate description. However, we are learning quickly.

FIVE

THE AGE OF WOMAN

In *What about Me?*, I described how the 'greed is good' ideology of the past 25 years has coloured our relations. What I didn't mention is that this ideology is just one more form of patriarchal, phallic authority. 'Phallic' will appear suspicious to some readers — Freud again. I will save myself a lengthy explanation by quoting a piece of conventional wisdom: every man wants to have the biggest, and this results in a pecking order.

'Where are our girls who blush gently, lower their heads, and turn their eyes away when we look at their face?' These are the words of the Turkish deputy prime minister Bülent Arinç in an address to mark the end of Ramadan in 2014. His speech lamented the 'moral decline of society'. Thousands of Turkish women reacted in defiance by posting pictures on the internet of themselves laughing uproariously. I've mentioned the story of the Emperor's new clothes; in practice, it's usually women who take on the role of the boy who spoke out, despite the fact that exposing the ruler is not without its dangers.

The history of the patriarchy is the history of the

oppression of women — sexually, intellectually, politically, and economically. There's a direct line from the witch hunts of the Middle Ages to the hysterics of the 19th century.[1] Until very recently, patients in psychiatric institutions came largely from two sections of the population: the lower social classes, and women. It's no accident that these are both groups that are at the bottom of the pyramid. In a painfully beautiful book, *Mad, Bad, and Sad: a history of women and the mind doctors*, Lisa Appignanesi describes the history of psychiatry as a history of male psychiatrists working above and against female patients. For those who think that such things are now in the past: the three young Russian women from Pussy Riot, who publicly protested against Vladimir Putin with playful acts of rebellion, were not only sentenced to serve time in a prison camp, but also given a psychiatric diagnosis, a 'combined personality disorder', explained in the legal report on the case as 'a condition that included different combinations of a "proactive approach to life", "a drive for self-fulfilment", "stubbornly defending their opinion", "inflated self-esteem", "inclination to opposition behaviour", and "propensity for protest reactions"'.[2]

Emancipation and awareness via a horizontal collective

The success of women's emancipation is down to a combination of various factors: the courage of individual women who took leading roles, scientific progress leading to the discovery of contraceptives, the decline of paternalistic religion, and universal access to education leading to better job opportunities. This created an awareness, in all kinds of groups and organisations, that the prevailing female roles (and therefore also male ones) were no more than just that, roles, and that they were being played out in the function of a particular social system which heavily discriminates against one half of the population.

The idea of gender roles tallies with my view of identity as a collection of social relations that we adopt via identification. As long as the patriarchy retained its dominant position, those social relations were taken for granted. Many people believed that they arose from 'human nature' (according to social Darwinism, women are weaker and less intelligent than men) or that they were determined by God (according to the creation story, woman is the source of original sin). These social relations were an irrefutable reality, and anyone who ran counter to them was seen as a heretic, as 'unnatural' or irrational. Yet the speed with which these roles have changed in recent decades proves otherwise. The realisation that they were merely roles, imposed by the existing social order and the corresponding authority, opened the way for other interpretations.

The way in which new interpretations gain acceptance illustrates the new way authority works. The old, wrong way still happens today, with well-meaning but nonetheless patronising attempts to force emancipation on women. Girls must attend co-educational schools; hijabs and chadors are condescendingly tolerated, or forbidden by law. This results in some women refusing an education and demanding their right to wear a chador or niqab. A harrowing example from the last century is the British colonial government's ban on female genital mutilation (FGM) in Sudan. This led to an increase in the number of women undergoing the procedure, out of protest against British rule ... A century later, it's the women themselves who, with the Somali Women's Democratic Organisation, are campaigning for the abolition of FGM. Now that women can decide for themselves, their attitude has completely changed.[3]

Mandatory emancipation is an example of paternalism: we know what's best; the others are stupid or immature. The underlying authority remains patriarchal, and, despite the apparent progressiveness, it changes little or nothing in reality. Emancipation from below does work, when a group of more-or-less-similar people — in this case, women — hold up a new mirror to others like them. Their authority is no longer based on a 'father knows best' model, but on a horizontal collective. This is the way in which second-wave feminism worked. Between roughly 1960 and 1980, women met in local groups to discuss what they themselves thought was important, and what changes they wanted to see. It is from this period that the expression 'the personal is political' dates.*

Such groups wielded a great deal of influence, precisely

---

* It was also in this period that so-called 'civil society' (the area of society that lies between citizens and their government) received fresh impetus. Associations became smaller in scale, gradually freed themselves from tradition, and went in search of new

because they functioned horizontally. Women were made aware by other women of the identity imposed on them, and they then set out together on the search for new interpretations, which they were then able to pass on to yet other women. Incidentally, those new interpretations can be extremely diverse. Letting go of a dominant, top-down dictated identity makes variety possible; it's a rejection of uniformity. There are multiple ways a woman can be emancipated. The main one is through education.

The education gap

Until the middle of the last century, women faced dual discrimination in education. Higher education was reserved almost exclusively for the upper classes and for boys. After World War II, this changed rather quickly, and school gates were opened to all children. In this case, 'all children' meant mainly boys; for another generation, girls had to be content with lessons in 'housekeeping'. Some trained to be teachers — a profession they were allowed to pursue as long as they remained unmarried. Nursing was another option, albeit invariably under the wing of a matron. Stewardess was a third, and more glamorous, possibility, but this glamour betrays a deep sexism, since stewardesses were judged on their appearance and could only continue to work in the job until they reached a certain age.[4]

In the last quarter of the 20th century, the number

interpretations of their own. We see the same processes happening again now.

of female students in general secondary education and higher education increased year by year, eventually closing the education gap between boys and girls. At my own university (Ghent), the pivotal year was 1995, with an equal number of female and male first-year students.[5] Now, Ghent University has its first female chancellor.

The current ratio of female to male students in higher education is three to two. Throughout Europe, there are currently on average 10 per cent more women with a university degree than men. Norway tops the charts with a difference of 18 per cent. In view of the gender distribution among current students, this gap can only increase, and the following comparison makes that clear: in the year 2000, 50.1 per cent of Belgians with a university degree were female; in the Netherlands, that figure was 54.8 per cent. By 2009, the figure in Belgium had risen to almost 55 per cent, and in the Netherlands to 56.5 per cent.[6] Furthermore, the 'economic return' on female students is considerably higher (they finish their studies more quickly and with better grades). The only remaining preserve of male (numerical) dominance among academic disciplines is in the engineering sciences (one woman for every five men). The education gap is no longer closed; it has reopened, but now in the other direction. More and more boys are failing to get a degree, and the traditional image of the highly educated man (lawyer, doctor, engineer) married to a less-well-educated woman (secretary, nurse, teacher) is beginning to flip.

This turnaround is now extremely apparent in the United States, because the trend began there ten years earlier. During the second wave of emancipation in the last century, American universities took measures to enable girls to enter higher education more easily. In recent years, they have reintroduced the same relaxation of admission procedures, but this time for boys, due to the drastic fall in the number of male students. This relaxed admissions policy has been introduced more or less in secret; apparently, it's politically sensitive.[7]

The education gap is growing due to a phenomenon that can be observed throughout Western societies: boys are performing increasingly badly at school. Compared to girls, they have more 'disorders', they have more attention-deficit problems, and they require more 'motivating'. The image of an older brother who brings his little sister safely to school — still the image on Belgian traffic signs to warn motorists that they are near a school — is clearly outmoded. Now, daughters have taken on the mantle of role model, and it's sons who give their mothers headaches. In his novella *My Dog Stupid*, John Fante tells the story of a teacher who gives a male pupil an F for a plagiarised essay, while, in a separate letter, he congratulates the boy's mother on the best piece of writing he's ever read. The number of mothers who do their sons' homework is greater than we think.

Why boys do less well than girls at school is difficult to ascertain. Compared to female students, males in higher education spend more time playing video games, partying, and pursuing sex. That's not sufficient as an explanation, however, because the fact is that most boys fall behind much earlier in their school careers. No one has come up with a clear explanation for this.[8]

The numerical dominance of female students in higher education results in more and more women entering high-level jobs. This development is progressing more slowly than expected — resistance to women at the top remains stiff, and it's very likely that quotas will be required to achieve a gender balance in traditional bastions of masculinity such as politics. In addition, women still almost always receive less pay than men for the same work.

This sluggish progress is often cited as proof of the indestructability of the patriarchy. There's supposed to be an unbreakable 'glass ceiling', an 'old boys' network' blocking women's rise. But those 'old boys' are indeed mostly old. In roughly half a century, the number of highly educated women and women in senior positions has surpassed the number in the entire previous 2500 years taken together, and the numbers continue to rise. In another quarter of a century, men at the top will have become a rare species in need of protection.

The gap between lower and higher education is closely connected to the gap between lower and higher income, and increasingly even with the gap between having a job and not having one. The vast majority of the low-skilled workforce is male, and, in our knowledge-driven economy, there are fewer and fewer jobs for such workers. In the lower classes, and increasingly also in the middle class, women (usually with a higher level of education than their partner) are often the main, or even the only, breadwinners, which is also a reversal of traditional roles. The effect this has on the shape of the modern family now closely follows the dividing line between social classes.

At the lower end of society, unemployed men have a greater tendency to cling on to traditional roles, while the woman-breadwinner no longer accepts that the father of her children should be the boss. The number of single mothers continues to rise, either because the father never accepted the paternal role or because the mother herself rejected him as a partner and a father for her children. Within this group, fewer and fewer women are opting to get married. In 2011, half of the births in the United States were to unmarried mothers below the age of 30. These women prefer to take charge of their own lives, usually without a man permanently by their side, and often with a mutual support network of other women. Their views on love and sex tend to be rather cynical in nature. The same trend can be seen in Europe. One child in every three is born out of wedlock; one in seven is born into a one-parent family. The future is likely to bring more of the same. In the Netherlands, it's estimated that 22 per cent of families will include only one parent by the year 2030.[9]

By contrast, there's a resurgence of marriage among the highly educated. After the 'flower power' generation, marriage became taboo for this group. Now, it's fashionable once again, but marriage has been reinterpreted. Both spouses are highly educated, although more and more female university graduates are marrying men with a lower level of education than theirs. Ideally, both have a well-paid job and they share the housework — ideally, because in practice childcare still ends up being mainly the responsibility of the woman/mother. Research in the US shows that this discrimination is now disappearing, and Europe is experiencing the same trend, although it can more accurately be described as a shift: housework remains underpaid work, now performed by female immigrants.

Despite the new success of marriage among the educated, the number of single people in that group is rising sharply, often by conscious choice. It's more than clear that something is changing in our love relationships.

I can do it without you

To judge by current divorce statistics, lasting relationships have become a great deal rarer than they used to be. Every magazine runs an article every few weeks in which a scientist explains the reason for this. Clinical psychologists claim that young people have difficulty committing to a partner because the relationships of their parents, the baby boomers, failed so often. Evolutionary psychology asserts that men are from Mars and women are from Venus, and 'never the twain shall meet'. There may be some truth in that, but the most obvious explanation for the rise in divorce rates is less complex and has mainly to do with the changes that have taken place in society over the past 50 years. The combination of a constantly increasing number of highly educated women, more economic independence, and the wide availability of reliable contraception has fundamentally changed the power relations between men and women. We can trace this development by looking at the blockbuster movies of two generations ago and comparing them to the latest trend at the cinema box office.

The romantic image is that of a knight in shining armour, who arrives on a white charger and saves the princess in distress. Since the 1980s, that traditional image has been spiced with a generous portion of eroticism, which serves to strengthen another cliché: men are mainly out to get laid, while women use their bodily charms to get ahead in life. At the beginning of *An Officer and a Gentleman*, the trainee naval officers are told that the local beauties all dream of becoming the wife of a fighter pilot and will even get pregnant on purpose to trap them into marriage. A man, on the other hand, a *real* man, gets ahead through hard work. Zack Mayo (played by Richard Gere) tries to get rid of his tattoos (which betray his origins) at the start of his hyper-strict officer training course. In the romantic final scene, we see him striding through a factory in his pristine white navy uniform, to the strains of 'Up Where We Belong' in the background, to rescue his princess from her life of drudgery. He is truly 'an officer and a gentleman', and there was not a dry eye in the house. This film — together with *E.T.* and *Tootsie* — was the box-office hit of the year (1982: the year of the officer, the alien, and the cross-dresser).

Eight years later, the same Richard Gere played the role of Edward Lewis, a jaded businessman, in *Pretty Woman*. At the start of the film, Lewis has literally lost his way and asks a woman (Vivian Ward, played by Julia Roberts) for directions. The woman appears — what a coincidence — to be a prostitute (it goes without saying that she's on the game for a noble cause: to pay her college fees). Lewis hires her for the night, and later for the entire week, and discovers not only the length of her legs, but also her inner beauty. He loses her after a predictable misunderstanding, but all's well that ends well, and he overcomes his fear of heights and climbs a fire escape — with a bunch of roses in his hand — to reach her at her window, where he asks for her hand in marriage. Earlier in the movie, Vivian had clearly stated what she expected: 'I want the fairy tale.'

Seven years earlier, a British film conveyed a very different message. *Educating Rita* shows a hairdresser (played by Julie Walters) together with her husband and her parents, clearly members of the British working class, drinking and singing in a dingy pub. Her mother is crying ('Why are you crying, Mother?' 'Because — because, there must be better songs to sing than this.'). Rita is criticised for not having got pregnant yet, which her husband Denny takes as a personal insult. But Rita has other plans: she wants to sing a better song, and signs up for a degree course at the Open University. When she meets her university tutor Dr Bryant (played by Michael Caine), she enters a different world. It's striking that the man does not appear as the saving angel; the woman takes the initiative for her own further education, and rather than a valiant knight, she meets a washed-up alcoholic academic. Her reaction to his cynicism can be read as the reaction of a new generation of women:

> I'll tell you what you can't bear, Mr Self-pitying Piss Artist. What you can't bear is that I'm educated now. I've got what you have, and you don't like it. I mean, good God, I don't need you.

> I've got a room full of books! I know what wine
> to buy, what clothes to wear, what plays to see,
> what papers and books to read, and I can do it
> without you.

Educating Rita is a story of emancipation from the 1980s, and so was ahead of its time. The expression 'I can do it without you' is the guiding principle of recent blockbusters with female lead characters within a totally different set of male–female relations. Beatrix 'The Bride' Kiddo (Uma Thurman's character in *Kill Bill*) leaves her employer and former lover Bill, whose baby she is carrying. He tries to murder her in revenge. She survives the attempt and will eventually kill the father of her child. In *The Girl with the Dragon Tattoo*, Lisbeth Salander (played by Noomi Rapace) takes revenge on her father and, more broadly, on all the abusive men around her. Furthermore, she rescues the male lead character when he's in danger of falling victim to a pervert who's been raping and murdering women for years. Jennifer Lawrence plays Katniss Everdeen in *The Hunger Games*, a young woman who's chosen to take part in a 'game' organised by the government, in which 12 young people are forced to fight to the death. Katniss not only kills all her opponents, but also saves her male comrade. And he is in love with her, although she does not return the sentiment.

We are now a world away from the two most famous women in 19th-century literature, *Anna Karenina* (Tolstoy) and *Madame Bovary* (Flaubert), for both of whom suicide was the only escape from their romantic failures. Yet 400 years earlier, Cervantes had already burst the bubble of romanticism with his tale of *Don Quixote*, a knight who battles dragons to impress his beloved maiden, Dulcinea. The dragons turn out to be windmills, Dulcinea is an ordinary barmaid, and the knight is nothing if not errant.

Today's knights are not only errant, but also afraid.

Who's afraid of Virginia Woolf?

The popular version of evolutionary psychology has instilled the following belief in many people: men are hypercompetitive and aggressive by nature, fighting with other males to spread their genes (their seed). The fact that they no longer compete on the savanna but on the stock market makes little difference. Women are more reserved, less aggressive by nature, tending more towards consultation and conciliation. The hope is that, now that women are increasingly taking on leadership positions, we will evolve into a better society.

I hold out that hope, too — but if it comes true, it will not be because of some sort of supposed feminine gentleness. In the US, the number of violent crimes committed by female adolescents has risen drastically (although boys are still significantly more prone to violence). At the same time, we're seeing a fall in the rate of violence *against* women and a rise in domestic violence *by* women. We can mothball the rose-tinted image of a gentle society run by women. Women can be aggressive, too. Social psychology experiments show that aggression in women is most likely to come to the fore when social expectations of women as 'soft' and 'conciliatory' are removed.[10]

When female identity changes, male identity must follow, since the two influence each other. When women were mostly housewives, their husbands mostly worked outside of the home. When women began to go out to work more, this relation changed. The demise of the patriarchy means that men have lost their privileged position and must now look for a new interpretation of their role. That loss causes fear, and the predictable reaction is a 'fight or flight' response.

There's a perception that men currently remain adolescent longer than women: they become independent (complete their education or training, move out of their parents' home, earn an independent income, and get a steady job) later than they used to, and later than their current female peers. It remains unclear whether men have more fear of commitment than their female counterparts — despite the fact that many women are convinced that this is the case. There may be any number of reasons why men remain single. For some, it's because they have more than an adequate supply of sex partners; for others, it may be that they're afraid of women. The latter group now has a name in Japan — *sōshoku(-kei) danshi*, or herbivore men — men who dare not enter into a relationship with a woman. They are thought to account for up to one-third of adolescents and two-thirds of unmarried adult men.[11]

During the hyper-patriarchal Victorian era, Freud described a typical solution for the conflict between the sexual urge and fear in men: tender love was reserved for a man's respectable wife; aggressive sex was for the inferior whore. The internet has given a new form to that dichotomy. Many psychologically intimate relationships remain in the virtual world of email, chat, texting, and webcams while the couples avoid actually meeting in the real world. At the other extreme, there's 'hook-up culture', sex with no emotional strings attached, as the newest version of the one-night stand (there really doesn't need to be a night involved; waking up next to a stranger is no big deal). This trend began in the colleges of America, where students — initially mainly men, but now also more and more women — go in search of sex without attachment, with the focus on enjoyment. A relationship is for later; first comes the career.[12]

Men's fear of women is an old subject — even, and perhaps especially, in the heyday of the patriarchy. From a psychoanalytical point of view, there are two explanations for it. The first is based on the idea that children see their mothers as all-powerful, and this omnipotence engenders fear of them. Fear of the mother expands into fear of women in general. Daughters can escape this by later becoming women/mothers themselves. In sons, the fear is reinforced by the fact that they become sexually dependent on women as adult men. In this context, men are the ones who are in the more supplicant position, hence the saying *ce que femme veut, Dieu le veut*, a woman's will is God's will.

The second explanation focuses on men. For centuries in Western culture, sexuality has been heavily suppressed, and portrayed as evil, reprehensible, or dangerous. For the dominant gender group — that is, men — the easiest way to control their own urges was through the oppression of women. In the religious context, Eve was given the blame. Women are identified as the source of original sin, and the best way for men to tackle the threat posed by their own sinful sexuality was to combat it within women, thereby avoiding having to fight it within themselves. This fight was given a social character, and the patriarchy enshrined the suppression of and aggression towards women in a range of social rules, from a ban on education for girls to mandatory 'modest' dress (and, of course, a separate area in the church, synagogue, or mosque).

The disappearance of the patriarchy and the male privilege it entails may offer an explanation for both men's fear of and overt aggression towards women. Structural aggression (denying women the vote, limiting women's access to education) has now more or less disappeared (FGM is a crime, mandatory 'modest' dress is heavily criticised, and education for women has become the norm). Violence towards women is now more the exception than the rule, and therefore receives more attention when it happens, which in turn can create the impression that there is now *more* aggression than before.

Probably, there is more fear, which in this context has much to do with sex.

Sex and power

Patriarchal authority stifles sexuality. Sex is bad, immoral, reprehensible — and the same is true of women, since they provoke men's sexual desires. By assigning gender positions in this way, the patriarchal system unintentionally vested women with a considerable amount of power, from the femme fatale to 'not tonight, dear, I have a headache'. This power offers another explanation for male aggression towards women.

Sex as a weapon. *La Source des Femmes* (*The Wellspring of Women*; distributed as *The Source* in English-speaking countries) is a film set in a North African Muslim country and tells the story of village women who protest against their circumstances using the oldest weapon at a woman's disposal: a sex strike. They resolutely keep their legs together until their menfolk begin to act more reasonably. The movie is a modern version of a 2500-year-old comedy. In Aristophanes' *Lysistrata*, all the women of Greece withhold sexual privileges from their men until they stop warring. The men negotiate a peace treaty in no time.

Sex as a weapon has become outdated, because our attitude to sexuality has completely changed thanks to emancipation and the pill. In the history of mankind, it's only in the past half-century that women have been able to enjoy carefree sex — and therefore to lust after it unequivocally.* As soon as the connection between sex and

---

* The contraceptive pill has a little-known dark side: a not-uncommon side effect is that that it suppresses sexual desire. This is even more true of antidepressants, which are also prescribed in huge numbers for women. This turns the myth of the woman who is never 'in the mood' into a pharmacological reality. But never worry, Big Pharma is already working hard to find a pill that will stimulate female sexual desire. I'm sure women will soon be able to buy all three pills together in a value pack.

pregnancy was cut, the link between sex, age, and gender also became considerably looser. Sex is not restricted to the years in which we're able to reproduce; we begin much earlier and continue for as long as we can. Eroticism is also now no longer restricted to married life or even to a pairing of man and woman of approximately the same age. Older women do it with much younger men and vice versa. Sex between people of the same gender is no longer taboo. Both men and women now have more sex with more different partners than they did in the past. As a result, sex has lost some of its leverage. Women can also be the initiators now, and this can also place men in a position of power.

The West has now seen the first generation of women for whom sex was no longer a source of fear. The effects of this are unmissable. Women go out looking for a partner for themselves, and they take a clearly active role during the sex act itself. The fact that many men don't know how to handle this shows how much they still cling to the double standards of the patriarchy (a sexually active man is a player; his female counterpart is a slut). Anyone who thinks this is no longer true of emancipated men in the West should watch Sunny Bergman's documentary film *Sletvrees* (*Slut Phobia*).[13]

The disappearance of patriarchal authority has without doubt been liberating as far as sex is concerned. Some people, however, view this liberation as a moral disaster and see it as the reason why two out of three marriages fail and why establishing relationships is so difficult. What they fail to realise is that the explanation for this lies elsewhere, for example in enforced individualisation and the free-market principles imposed on us, even in our relationships. We 'invest' in relationships on a marriage market (who is the best buy?). Choosing a partner often takes place via online dating, where there might always be a higher ranked potential candidate who corresponds to our desired profile — so we keep swiping, with the eventual result that we end up alone. We forget that we choose our partners according to gut feeling, and not on the basis of rational considerations. Mr Spock from *Star Trek* ('live long and prosper'), *the* prototype of a rational being, is undoubtedly both single and childless by choice.

Another reason for the rising number of single people lies in the autonomy that's imposed on us — everyone is expected to 'do their own thing'. The American sociologist Richard Sennett notes that the all-pervasive emphasis on the individual, and the associated emphasis on psychological analysis of our lives, makes us forget that we are, first and foremost, social creatures. The fact that we need contact with others is something we no longer care to admit. Everyone is on a search to find him- or herself, as an individual. But this quest can never end with a satisfactory result, due to the nature of the quest itself. As an individual, I am nobody; my identity only acquires meaning in relation to others.

On top of this emphasis on the individual and the psychological, we also see a hyper-eroticisation of society (sex sells), which Sennett sums up rather drily as follows: 'we unendingly and frustratingly go in search of ourselves through the genitals'.[14] Unfortunately, with a new kind of dissatisfaction as a result.

Gender

The patriarchal system is based on a sharply delineated binary division of gender: you are either a man or a woman. Binary categories have a striking feature. One of the two poles is superior, the other inferior; one is dominant, the other passive (man/woman, nature/culture, body/mind …). A reversal is always possible (in contrast to the past, the body is now more important than the mind, 'everything' is determined by our genes, and psychologists can't turn to neuroscience quick enough), but that doesn't do anything to change the system itself.

Either man or woman. And one always attracted to the other. Until not so long ago, homosexual people had to conceal their desires, often by entering into a heterosexual marriage. In his play *Passions humaines*, the Flemish writer Erwin Mortier describes the loving relationship between the novelist Georges Eekhoud and the socialist Sander Pierron at the end of the 19th century. Both were married men, and their letters to each other were not discovered until 1992. From the Middle Ages, homosexuality was punishable by death, and the last execution for homosexuality in the Netherlands was carried out in 1803.[15] Under the influence of the French Revolution, homosexuality was eventually removed from the criminal code, only to appear in psychiatric handbooks instead. It wasn't until 1990 that the World Health Organisation removed homosexuality from its list of psychiatric disorders. Homosexual people can be as (ab)normal as heterosexuals — and they are just as diverse. The first same-sex marriage allowed by national law took place in the

Netherlands in 2001, and many countries have followed suit in legalising marriage equality since then.

Natural and unquestioning acceptance of the gender binary division had to be reassessed when a differentiation began to be made between 'sex' (biological fact) and 'gender' (the psychological feeling of belonging to a particular sexual group) and 'sexuality'. As a result of this, categories of psychosexual identity had to be extended to include not just male and female, but also homosexual and bisexual. Later, transgender and intersex were also recognised. One of the principle effects of this broadening of the categories of sexuality was to blur the sharp boundaries between different identities.

This development called into question the generally accepted argument that biology determines psychosexual identity characteristics. In the classical view, a woman was 'typically feminine' (gentle, maternal, a little bit naive, conciliatory), and a man was 'typically masculine' (competitive, aggressive, hierarchical, results-oriented). In the last quarter of the previous century, biological determination was put increasingly in doubt as research showed that such characteristics can mainly be attributed to upbringing and culture, as coloured by the patriarchy.

This assertion has been increasingly confirmed since then. For the past decade, in the wake of the rise of brain research, scientists have been searching eagerly for neurological differences between men and women. And indeed, male and female brains don't appear to be completely identical. However, the link between the brain and psychological gender traits is anything but clear and, in my opinion, not really convincing. There's far more evidence to show that the gender differences that supposedly originate in biology are actually more closely connected to social expectations. In 1974, American psychologist Sandra Bem designed a self-rating scale that aimed to measure the extent to which a person has certain psychological characteristics that are seen as typically feminine or masculine. A comparison of modern results and those from the past reveals that women now exhibit considerably more 'masculine' traits. The opposite is also true, but to a lesser extent. The most important conclusion from this is that such traits are not at all associated with masculinity or femininity by dint of their nature, but as a result of social expectations. Compared to 1974, those expectations are now very different, which is the explanation for the shift in the results of Bem's test.

The sharp division between men and women fitted very well into the patriarchal model, in which men and fathers were automatically afforded a higher and better position than the 'weaker sex'. The birth of a son was good news, but the arrival of a daughter was a disappointment. Following the decline of the patriarchy, young people now grow up in a culture where sexual orientation is on a spectrum (straight, gay, bi) and doesn't immediately conjure up ideas of certain associated psychological traits. Heterosexual men come in all sorts of shades and hues, just like homosexual women, for example, and both have to wrestle with culturally determined expectations. These days, those expectations have much to do with the hyper-individualisation of society and with the excessive emphasis placed on our professional lives. This can be the source of many problems for those who want to have children and a career.

'The family'

Indeed, 'the family' — in quotation marks, to show the word now retains little of its traditional meaning. The family albums of yesteryear often showed a mildly bored father, a proud mother, and a number of children. Looking at family photos today on an iPad, you see a very different picture. 'That's me with my real father, and here I am with Mum and her new boyfriend and his kids, and this is me with my girlfriend. We're thinking of having kids, too. She's going to get pregnant first and then it'll be my turn. We've agreed that I should concentrate on my career first.'

The traditional family has now become the exception rather than the rule. Divorce rates are very high, and fewer and fewer people are getting married; stepfamilies and one-parent families are becoming the norm.[16] There are various reasons for this, and they have a great deal to do with the decline of traditional authority. Everybody used to be expected to tie the knot, not having children was a disaster or suspicious, and divorce was a disgrace. Men married to gain morally acceptable access to sex and got a housekeeper into the bargain. Women married in the hope of having children and a good breadwinner (owning a house was the main ambition). Now, it's often men who want to have children, and if sex is still an issue within marriage, it's mainly as a reason to separate.

A consideration of our modern vocabulary of the

family shows this new diversity: we have nuclear families, extended families, single-person households, living apart together (LAT), living together apart (LTA), reconstituted families, rainbow families, patchwork families, astronaut families, family of choice, and so on, and so on. It's a nightmare for lawyers (how to draw up a will for a family that has been reconstituted three times?). For the family members — whatever form their 'family' takes — the challenges are always the same. How to combine personal and professional life? How to combine having a career and having kids? How to combine a lasting relationship with a desire for passion in your life? These questions are by no means new, but they are now just as relevant for women as they always have been for men.

In the past, a woman's success depended on the man she was married to. This is still the case today, but for a totally different reason. How willing is a woman's partner to take on some of the housework? Whose career gets priority? A young woman with an ambitious careerist as her partner will usually have to put her own ambitions to one side. The opposite is true, too, but househusbands remain the exception. The demands of the labour market place a lot of pressure on our private lives, and if both partners want to pursue their careers, their partnership is forced to become a relationship of convenience.

Recently, Femma (an influential Flemish women's group) called for a reduction in working hours. The proposal was immediately shot down by the male head of the business organisation Unizo. According to him, we work far too little, 'growth' is the magic word, and we all need to work harder.

This dialogue of the deaf illustrates the sharp distinction between a man who is blindly clinging to a world that's busy destroying itself, and a woman who has recognised the situation for what it is and is looking for answers.

The world of fixed working hours, in which working for longer was called 'overtime' (and paid double, no less) is more or less a thing of the last century. Now, professionals may easily work 50 hours a week, while more and more low-skilled workers hold down two jobs to make ends meet, a large number of people are stuck in long-term unemployment, and we all swallow masses of pills just to keep going.

Based on the rising figures for absenteeism from work due to sickness, and the increase in cases of executive burnout, this 'keeping going' is becoming more and more difficult. The most obvious solution is to redress the balance between work and income, which would put more people in work and make combining personal and professional life possible again. This solution is a result of the 'thinking outside the box' that politicians and economists love to talk about so much. In reality, they just repeat the old solutions ('More growth!', 'Work harder!', 'Work longer!') to the new problems (long-term unemployment for one group, executive burnout for the other) that arise as a consequence of their rehashed solutions.

Meanwhile, it's often the man in a relationship who is keen to have a baby (this is also true of a second child). Highly educated women are certainly putting on the brakes, or even choosing to remain childless. Women know only too well that the parenting responsibilities will end up in their lap, even if their partner means well. There has been a noticeable shift when it comes to children: in the West, the preference is no longer automatically for sons, but increasingly for daughters. In cases where this choice can be made actively (adoption or artificial insemination with sperm selection), there's an overwhelming preference for daughters.[17]

The pressures of today's labour market undoubtedly create problems when it comes to childcare. The number of hours that parents spend outside the home due to work has increased inexorably; the number of childcare facilities (creches, preschools, schools, after-school care) has fallen, and they have become more expensive. Many a child begins and ends his or her life on a waiting list. As a baby, this means waiting for a place in a creche; as an old person, this often means waiting until it's too late to get a room in a care home — and both places are extremely expensive.* As a working adult, you have to earn an unusually high salary to afford to have children. And the price you pay is that you hardly ever see them.

Fathers and mothers aren't just fathers and mothers; they're also men and women (by extension, the same is true of same-sex parents). Combining our sexual and parental

---

* The Scandinavian countries show that this can be handled differently. Their childcare is among the best in the world, parental leave is shared equally by both parents, and the costs are covered almost entirely by the government. Yes, their taxation levels are very high and result in an equitable redistribution of income, with very transparent use of tax money.

roles isn't easy, and a long-term cohabiting relationship is a passion killer. Compared to the past, we enjoy much greater sexual freedom, and that's true most of all for women. But how can that be combined with parenthood? How can we combine this freedom with the desire for continuity? It's blatantly obvious that human beings are not biologically monogamous, but, against our better judgement, most of us continue to expect sexual exclusivity of our partners. A new kind of double standard has arisen, whereby women, too, often maintain more than one relationship at the same time, and they, too, have trouble accepting the same behaviour from their partners.

Horizontal authority

The patriarchal system operates in a pyramidal structure, with the army and the church as illustrations of this. There are barely any female equivalents, which is an indication that this kind of structure is less prevalent among groups of women. Now that the patriarchy is on the wane and more and more highly educated women are taking up leadership positions, some people dream of a gentler, female-dominated society based on supposedly typical feminine traits like empathy, a focus on consultation, and a long-term view.

This hope is an ancient one. At the end of his career, the same Aristophanes who wrote about the women's sex strike also wrote a comedy in which women take an even more dominant position: *Ecclesiazusae*, often translated into English as '*A Parliament of Women*'. In this play, the women of Athens use a trick to vote themselves into power, since the men are failing to rule properly — they are only interested in feathering their own nests and are ruining the city in the process. As soon as the women take over the parliament, they bring in some radical changes. Marriage is abolished (anyone can sleep with anyone else, but beautiful people must sleep with everyone who is uglier than them before they can have sex with their equals in pulchritude) and wealth is redistributed equally among all citizens.

In May 2013, female students at Stanford University adapted Aristophanes' play to modern times. In their version, women seize economic power to stop 'the power patriarchy of Oldman Sacs Inc.' from ruining the world any further.[18] Michael Young — the man who predicted with uncanny accuracy the rise of what we now call neoliberalism in *The Rise of the Meritocracy 1870–2033* (a science fiction story written in 1958) — suggests that a rebellion by highly educated women will bring that system down. And in a recent management book written by two men, the authors predict that women will soon run the world, making it a much better place.[19]

I doubt this view very much. It's certainly true that characteristics such as empathy and a focus on consultation, combined with a long-term view, can create a better society, but the question is whether these really are typically feminine traits. Strangely enough, the idea of a society run exclusively by women often elicits very negative reactions from women themselves. One of my female associates expressed it in terms that would cost a man his head: 'Women can be really nasty to other women, and they *never* forget what another woman has done to them.'

Both personal experience and academic research reveal that teams with approximately the same number of male and female members work better than single-sex teams. There's little evidence that companies run by a woman, or with several women in top positions, do better than those with exclusively male executive boards.[20]

What I do believe is that the shape of the organisation is crucial. When authority operates according to a top-down pyramidal structure, it's not so important whether the pyramid is made up of men or women. In such a structure, those who climb the ladder will always be careerists, and female careerists certainly exist, too. An organisation with a horizontal structure requires different characteristics of its members, and this means a different sort of person will be pushed to the forefront. Such an organisation functions on the basis of horizontal leadership, allowing different people to take the lead in turn. The hierarchical aspect is minimal; the emphasis lies on coaching and consultation.

We're now seeing this trend in company management styles with names like 'shared leadership' and 'servant leadership'.[21] A group is no longer restricted to one leader; leadership can change as the different abilities of the group's members are required, while the common goal of the group always remains in the foreground. Businesses run in this way do better.

In the name of the father

The shift from top-down leadership towards shared decision-making is associated with a certain social change that also gets to the heart of the patriarchal system, namely the fact that parents can now choose which surname to give their children. Until recently, it was unthinkable that a child should bear the mother's surname except in very few cases (bastard child, incest) in which it was often associated with social stigma. Patrilineal descent was the only 'real' line; women were expected to bear children for fathers and for the fatherland. In many European countries, the patrilineal surname was even required by law. This is now a thing of the past, and women are just as likely as men to pass on their name to their children.

In the Netherlands, parents have been allowed to choose the surname of the father or the mother for their children since 1998; if they can't agree, the decision is made by a court judge. The Belgian regulations, which were not introduced until 2014, guarantee the right of the parents to choose their children's surnames; they can opt for a single surname (that of either parent) or a double-barrelled name combining both. Here, if the parents can't reach agreement, the child automatically receives the name of the father, which in effect gives the father a right of veto. The Belgian Institute for the Equality of Women and Men immediately filed a complaint against this regulation with the country's Constitutional Court. More or less the same thing happened in Germany, albeit a quarter of a century earlier, in 1991, when Germany's Federal Constitutional Court eliminated the dominance of the father in Germany's naming laws. But conservative groups in Belgium have even raged against the current regulations (even with a de facto right of veto for the father), and they are totally against adopting Germany's model. That's no wonder, since that decision was of historic scope. If Belgium's Constitutional Court removes the fathers' right of veto, the line of descent will no longer be exclusively male in yet another country, and it will sound the final death knoll for the patriarchy.[22]

SIX

PARENTS IN THE PLURAL

The connection between parenting and authority is so obvious that parenting is often held up as a natural model for authority, including in politics. 'Managing like a good housefather' is the slogan in Flanders. Note that authority in a parenting situation has a statutory time limit. In our modern constitutional state, a specific age limit is placed on it. At the age of 18, individuals are responsible for themselves and are expected to have sufficiently internalised a 'voluntary submission' to the prevailing rules of social interaction. In many countries, this majority coincides with the end of compulsory education, which is an indication of how closely connected parenting and education are.

In this 'natural' version of authority, parents take responsibility for their offspring until they reach ~~majority~~. *maturity* Authority clearly implies responsibility.

But responsibility for what? In the first place, responsibility for seeing that a child develops as well as possible. However, the responsibility of parents goes much further than that, because they must also teach their children about the expectations of, customs in, and obligations to the family, social class, and culture they're part of. Parents don't invent these themselves, but function as a conduit for what is customary. Expressed in somewhat solemn terms, they represent the law. This is more than just a figure of speech: parents are legally liable for the behaviour of their underage offspring.

By force of law — this is the difference from pure power. Society confers on parents a legally based authority over their children. If they fail to exercise that authority as they should, the law is equally able to take their children away ('relieve them of their parental rights'). Furthermore, they are subject to the law themselves and may be held accountable. Any parents who've had to pick their adolescent son up from the local police station will know what I mean.

Parenting and violence

What place do power and violence have in parenting and education? The question alone will send a shiver down many people's spines. Our abhorrence of violence combined with abuses of power mean we condemn it in any form. Political violence is unacceptable, punishment in the classroom scarcely more so, capital punishment is unthinkable, and even a parental clip round the ear is cause for concern. 'Violence is proof of impotence' is the truism of the day, proving that everyone thinks they're a psychologist. There may be some truth to it, but as a generalisation it is as naive as it is incorrect.

Violence is often an outright expression of power (just ask any women who has been raped). In our outrage, we often forget to ask the right questions. Is power exercised legitimately or not? Is the violence authorised — which means, is it based on authority that's underpinned by society? When the police use their batons in a heavy-handed way to keep a bunch of drunken hooligans in check, they're using an authorised form of violence. If they go too far, exceeding the limits of their authority, then they themselves are made to face the law by means of the appropriate control mechanisms.

Authority is not synonymous with power, let alone violence. Yet authority does have to do with force — at best, a force that works from the inside out; otherwise, it's a force that must be imposed from the outside by a legitimate body, which may be authorised to use violence. A law must be enforceable, otherwise it will be simply disregarded by everyone. Pascal understood this: 'Justice without might is helpless; might without justice is tyrannical. Justice without might is gainsaid, because there are always offenders ...'[1] A glance at history shows that every form of authority can be traced to an original form of violence. The Founding Fathers of America were terrorists who blew away the legal authority of the United Kingdom.

External force? An original form of violence? Any attempt to apply these to parenting and education immediately sparks outrage and conjures up images of crying children and sadistic parents wielding canes or whips. These are things that belong in the past. Parental love, and certainly maternal love, is unconditional, isn't it? This is an illusion we've inherited from romanticism, which in every possible key sang the praises of the mythical monogamous couple, eternally in love with each other, and the fable of unconditional maternal love (alas, the mother was often sickly and the beloved always unattainable).

Parental care is indeed almost completely unconditional in the first few months of our lives. We wake up hungry or in need of a nappy change, start to cry, and, as if by magic, someone appears at the cradle-side, takes us lovingly in their arms, coos comfortingly at us, and solves the problem. Two hours later, the scene repeats itself, with the same results, and so it goes on for a few months. This simple form of conditioning induces a spontaneous expectation that stays with us for the rest of our lives: when I have a problem, someone will appear and solve it for me. Going in search of a solution ourselves is something that comes later.

Searching ourselves for solutions is something we learn as children. That initially unconditional love ('Look what a mess she's making with her little spoon, so sweet!') will shift after about a year to a more conditional kind of love — 'If you do as Mummy says, Mummy will be nice to you; if you don't, Mummy will be angry.' This is the main form of 'violence' in parenting: withholding love, even to the point of rejection. This psychological form of violence has a far greater impact than a clip round the ear, and its coercive effect is much stronger. It can also take on a physical form that taps directly into our social nature: exclusion, removal from the safety of the group. 'Go stand in the corner!'

Such forms of psychological violence are part of

parenting, preferably in combination with loving attention paid to the behaviour and concepts we *do* want to see in our children. Even though some people don't want to hear it, parenting is manipulation. We think up all sorts of strategies to raise our children to live up to our best expectations. This won't happen by itself. In an ideal parenting situation, parents gradually allow their growing children to participate in decisions about what those expectations should be.

I can imagine that this claim — that parental authority is based on a form of violence — will be met with much opposition. Abhorrence of violence perpetrated by dictatorships (often called 'authoritarian regimes') is undoubtedly responsible for this attitude in part. However, I'm afraid that there can be no two ways about it: authority can only operate if it's supported by the possibility of legitimately exercised power and coercion. In normal circumstances, as little use as possible is made of this option. But loving attention will not teach a toddler that touching a hot oven can be painful and dangerous, and that crossing the road without looking is not a good idea. To learn such things, a toddler needs to hear repeated prohibitions, and, if necessary, to experience punishment if those prohibitions are violated. As such, I think a slap on the bottom is less dangerous than an unremitting form of psychological violence. Or, even worse, an extreme form of indifference and psychological neglect, often under the guise of a 'free' upbringing.

From anti-authoritarianism to psychotherapy as a disciplinary measure

After the horrors of World War II, authority gained an extremely negative connotation. First the right-wing dictatorships were unmasked, then the left-wing ones, and the free West had finally had a bellyful of the paternalistic meddling of church and state. Authority was bad; long live freedom, even at home and at school. In its pedagogical expression, this movement became known as anti-authoritarianism.

It's always easy to point out errors in retrospect. In that postwar era, 'authority' meant patriarchal authority, and it was not seen as distinct from power. The realisation that authority is indispensable in parenting and education hadn't yet pervaded popular opinion. There's not a single child who would understand without being told by an adult that drinking gallons of cola and eating mountains of fries is unhealthy. And very few children will 'motivate themselves' to tackle tough study material ('Hooray! Rote-learning multiplication tables!'). 'Applause parenting', which places no or very few demands on the child, isn't parenting at all. Paradoxically, this approach often leaves children with low self-esteem and a greater risk of problems in later life.[2] Parenting *is* making demands.

Which brings us to one of the problems of our times: the growing number of children whose behaviour is unmanageable, both at home and at school. The crucial point is discipline, or rather, the lack of it, even in 'normal' families and at 'normal' schools. This behaviour ranges from students refusing to participate in class to truancy, and from bullying of other children *and* teachers to truly antisocial behaviour, including physical aggression towards teaching staff. In their shared desperation, schools and parents have now discovered a new expert: the child psychologist.

Resorting to the psychologist is tempting, and it invokes ideas that no one could oppose: paying more attention to children as children; paying more attention to their emotional needs and individual problems; paying less attention to performance and competition; and putting less emphasis on acquiring knowledge for its own sake. A day at school for the little ones often begins with a group discussion where they can let off steam.[3] This gives the school a (pseudo)therapeutic function without anyone realising it. And — even more radically — the classroom becomes a diagnostic centre. This turns psychologists into the new authority, albeit with kid gloves, and in the name of science. Note that this means that schools and teachers, and even parents, willingly relinquish their authority. Just take a look at an advertising leaflet that was circulated in 2014 by a self-appointed team of 'Flemish child psychologists':

> KNOW YOUR CHILD
> Think of their future.
> Are you sure you know your child well enough?
> Do you have questions about your child's development?
> **We can help you answer them.**
> Only then can your child develop to their full potential.

WHAT WE DO

Academic results do not tell the whole story!
We examine whether your child is continuing to
develop well at school and at home.

We **answer** all your questions about parenting
and your child's psychological development.

CHILDREN GO TO THE DENTIST'S FOR A YEARLY CHECK-UP, SO SHOULDN'T THEY NEED A PSYCHOLOGICAL CHECK-UP, TOO?

A happy child is just as important as healthy
teeth.

WHO IS IT FOR?

Children aged between 6 and 16.

We come **to your home** (a safe environment for
your child), to school, or to the student guidance
centre. We arrange everything for you.

Let me dwell a little on that comparison with a visit to
the dentist. Medical professionals use objective standards
that are valid around the world, based on the biological
development of the human body. A yearly check-up is
a good idea. Parenting and psychological development
come on top of biological development, but there are few
objective measurements that can be made, although there

are many norms, in the moral meaning of the word.* This offer of a yearly check-up plays to the fear parents have about whether their child is properly equipped for today's rat race.

The sociologist Frank Furedi remarks that a crisis in education is often a symptom of a society in crisis. The age we live in is an illustration of this, and the result is an increasing number of children with difficulties. The most obvious approach should focus on the social context in which education takes place. However, that is rare, and the approach usually taken these days is well illustrated by the advertising leaflet. A subtle suggestion is made that a child may be slower than normal to develop, or even that they may have a disorder, and that a good parent must pay the necessary attention to this and have their child checked regularly.

There have never before been so many children with diagnostic labels, with the vague background belief that their diagnosed disorder is actually an illness. This confines the problem to the young, and by extension to their parents, while the broader social questions go ignored. Giving children a diagnostic label (which they are then

---

* Development psychology used to produce relatively value-free descriptions of the motor, sensor, verbal, emotional, and social development of babies, infants, and children. Now, its use has fallen prey to what I call the checklist approach, with an explicit normative impact. This may fit in with well-intentioned ideas such as 'early detection' or 'stepped care', but in practice the result is an all-pervasive labelling of children and constantly worried parents ('Lizzie is a little below average, but we're working on it!').

often burdened with for the rest of their school career) means treatment can be administered. Problems are turned into psychological issues, which have now become more or less synonymous with medical issues (pills are quickly prescribed). In just a short period of time, this approach has come to define our education system.

Many of these 'problem children' are indeed highly problematic, but to consider them *psychiatrically* disturbed makes a mockery of what psychiatry is supposed to be. If you think I'm exaggerating, just read the following:

Conduct Disorder

A repetitive and persistent pattern of behaviour in which the basic rights of others or major age-appropriate societal norms or rules are violated, as manifested by the presence of at least three of the following 15 criteria in the past 12 months from any of the categories below, with at least one criterion present in the past 6 months:

Aggression to People and Animals
1. Often bullies, threatens, or intimidates others.
2. Often initiates physical fights.
3. Has used a weapon that can cause serious physical harm to others (e.g., a bat, brick, broken bottle, knife, gun).
4. Has been physically cruel to people.
5. Has been physically cruel to animals.
6. Has stolen while confronting a victim

(e.g., mugging, purse snatching, extortion, armed robbery).

7. Has forced someone into sexual activity.

Destruction of Property

8. Has deliberately engaged in fire setting with the intention of causing serious damage.

9. Has deliberately destroyed others' property (other than by fire setting).

Deceitfulness or Theft

10. Has broken into someone else's house, building, or car.

11. Often lies to obtain goods or favours or to avoid obligations (i.e., 'cons' others).

12. Has stolen items of nontrivial value without confronting a victim (e.g., shoplifting, but without breaking and entering: forgery).

Serious Violations of Rules

13. Often stays out at night despite parental prohibitions, beginning before age 13 years.

14. Has run away from home overnight at least twice while living in the parental or parental surrogate home, or once without returning for a lengthy period.

15. Is often truant from school, beginning before age 13 years.

What you have just read is the official list of criteria for a psychiatric disorder, as described in the previously mentioned *Diagnostic and Statistical Manual of Mental Disorders*. The number of children and young people who receive this label is increasing hand over fist. Such 'diagnoses' are based solely on social norms, and thus on external criteria — in my view, they are pedagogical and legal judgements, not medical diagnoses. Well-nigh every study shows that young people who are labelled in this way exhibit increased anxiety, but, strangely, anxiety is not included in this so-called 'diagnostic' description.

This judgemental approach is symptomatic of a society that refuses to look to itself to find the blame. *They* are disturbed; *we* have nothing to do with it. Practically every problem teenager was raised in a traumatic environment, where authority was long-ago replaced by power. It becomes even more uncomfortable when we realise that their 'treatment' is often a replication of this situation and comes down to a barely concealed, power-based disciplinary measure ('Show him who's boss!'). This results in a spiral of violence, which only serves to increase the young person's difficulties (and our own). Once they are adults, the label changes to 'antisocial personality disorder', with prison as the final destination.

The media's inflation of these problems obscures the fact that these young people are in a minority (albeit a growing one). Ordinary students are still in the majority in schools. But it's often the 'ordinary' students who really get their teachers' goat. Furedi quotes one such teacher:

> It is the disrespect and the defiance that are the most difficult issues to deal with. It is the tap, tap, tap of the pen on the desk, the orchestrated coughing, the swinging back and forth on the

chair, the refusal to comply with the simplest
requests, wearing coats, hoodies, sunglasses, the
text messages and phone calls that disrupt lessons.[4]

Attempts to restore traditional authority to parenting
and education always fail, and the subsequent descent
into pure power simply makes the problems worse. We
must come up with a new solution, based on a different
interpretation of authority.

It takes a village to raise a child

As I've explained, in my view, the new basis for authority
is to be found in the group. If we apply that to parenting
and education, the solution appears to be — collective
parenting? — unrealistic and even undesirable. Parenting
is the exclusive task of parents, and how could such a group
be organised, anyway? It's clear that parents are and should
remain the most important people in the parenting process.
At the same time, we're living in a society in which parents
have less and less time to spend with their children, and
children are brought up from an early age by a more-or-
less-interrelated group of people: family members, but also
childminders, neighbours, anyone involved in education,
before- and after-school care, sports clubs, and let's not
forget the school bus driver. Rather than bewailing this
state of affairs, we can consciously embrace it as the source
of a new kind of authority.

This is the proposal made by Haim Omer, a professor
at Tel Aviv University. The new authority in parenting and

education lies with a collective that surrounds the child, and is new mainly because it doesn't attempt to restore the old version of itself. This renewal lies in the replacement of classic top-down authority with a horizontal version supported by many different people.

Omer describes in a very pragmatic way how parents and teachers can approach this. The intention is that parents can rely on, and themselves be part of a supportive collective. The same is true of educators, and, in ideal circumstances, parents and teachers can find each other in this network, together with the students themselves.[5]

This is the modern version of the old saying, 'It takes a village to raise a child.' In an age where one child in seven grows up in a one-parent family, parenting by a group is sorely needed.

Individual versus collective

Mark is 14 and has a reputation as a troublemaker both at school and in the neighbourhood. He bullies other children, fails to keep promises, and has already been caught stealing. His mother is ashamed, and tries to find excuses for his problems: 'Mark has had a difficult time of it since his father walked out.' The school has made repeated efforts to motivate him: 'Think of your future.' To no avail. Teachers are beginning to avoid Mark, but, after the umpteenth fight, Mr Peters is sick of Mark; he separates the two combatants and confronts Mark with his behaviour: 'You're always causing trouble, you little thug. It's high time you were …' Mark vehemently denies any wrongdoing, blames other children, and runs away.

In the weeks that follow, he becomes even more aggressive, but out of the teachers' sight, in places they almost never go. Other parents complain, a psychologist is called in, and a psychological examination results in the predictable label — conduct disorder. Mark's mother is called into school. She promises to cooperate but fails to mention that the situation at home is gradually becoming untenable — her son is now in charge of the living room and has control of the TV and the computer.

On the advice of the psychologist, 'agreements' are made, with clear penalties for Mark if he fails to keep to them. He promises to be good, but in the same week he punches another boy in the face, leaving him with a bloody nose. Mark is suspended from school for a week. On the third day of his suspension, the school psychologist has a talk with Mark's mother, who assures him her son is behaving well. Two days later, she phones the police in floods of tears, saying that Mark has hit her and run away from home.

A juvenile court judge decides to place Mark in an institution. His report says that Mark's mother lacks authority and his school can no longer cope with his behaviour.

This fictitious case illustrates just about everything that's wrong with our approach to problem teenagers. The parent is left alone, feels blamed, withdraws, and conceals information. The teenager is also alone; he is the problem. When confronted, he denies everything, his level of aggression increases, and the problems escalate. The police get involved, and he disappears from the community, only to return a few years later and cause even greater problems. This failure is perfectly predictable, and yet we still continue to cling on to this exclusively individual approach.

Mark's story might have been different if the approach described by Omer, based on the authority of a collective, had been followed. I deliberately used the phrase 'the authority of a collective' and not 'the authority of *the* collective'. This isn't a closed group, but a consciously selected collection of people (parents, class teachers, sports-club leaders, friends, and classmates …), who can come or go. Some are in a very central position (mostly the parents), and the initiative to act as a group comes from them. They invite the others to be part of the group, and have a very important function: making sure different members of the group communicate properly with one another.

Together, they all consistently communicate the same messages to the teenager *and* his or her broader environment (including his or her friends and their parents). They all hold up the same mirror. We then see presence instead of absence, difference and distance rather than equality, watchful concern rather than control, transparency rather than secrecy, rehabilitation rather than punishment. The authority that goes along with all this doesn't come from a lone super-parent or super-teacher, but is spread among various people. The force it commands has everything to do with social pressure and social control.

Presence through distance and difference

Authority operates on the basis of a voluntary submission, an inner compulsion. This comes about in young people only if they're confronted with expectations over a long-enough period. The requirements for this are obvious: the people presenting those expectations must actually be present. After a time, children take on the expectations, the external compulsion becomes internalised, and that concrete presence no longer need be so concrete.

Many parents shy away from adopting a position of authority, and are unwilling to communicate a clear 'no'. Some because they believe that it simply isn't right; others because they fear a rancorous reaction from their child. The combination of a lack of time and a difficulty with adopting a clear position of authority leads some to opt for a 'soft' approach. Their aim is to present themselves as friends and equals rather than authority figures. But in doing so, they are making a basic error: authority rests upon difference and distance. When a mum calls her 14-year-old daughter 'my best friend' or a Dad talks to his 12-year-old son 'man to man', they're creating an illusion of equality. Adolescents will quickly try to dominate in such a situation, with repeated conflicts as the result.

Conflict is precisely what such parents are out to avoid, and the easiest way to avoid rows is to further reduce their already reduced presence. This creates a vicious circle, with the most extreme result being that some parents are truly afraid of their children — and then the floodgates are well and truly open. For some time now, abuse of parents has no longer been restricted to the abuse of the elderly, and teachers have become afraid of psychological and even physical violence from some of their students.

This difficulty with adopting a clear position of authority, and the choice for a soft approach, is evident in many schools, too, with the same results. Teachers who are out to avoid conflict and who hope to solve everything by becoming friends with their students, through group discussions and suchlike, simply see their problems mounting. Consequently, they, too, try to limit contact with the children. The staffroom becomes a safe haven, playground supervision is like running the gauntlet, and certain places (bike sheds, toilets, behind the gym, the part of the playground that's out of sight) become no-go zones, where the students rule the roost. The power relations — there can no longer be any talk of authority — are reversed, and each conflict lays the foundation for the next.

Parenting and educating require distance, but that mustn't result in absence. Presence is necessary, with distance based on difference. My students aren't allowed to address me by my first name; I am not one of them, but they must feel able to address me per se. Parents and teachers need to reclaim their presence, and — most importantly — they must not do so alone. They should be present as members of a collective. Haim Omer calls this vigilant care.

Vigilant care in place of control

Control is impersonal, connected to power (command and control), and based on the threat of immediate intervention (usually punishment). Ideally, control is also total, which means it carries the seed of its own failure within it. The greater the number of control systems in place, the greater the risk of infringement — hyperbolic growth of control systems is indicative of the disappearance of authority and a lapse into pure power. As soon as the controlling figure turns around, those under his control mock him and consider launching their next challenge. Pure power incites challenge and escalation.

Authority is associated with time and sustainability, and very rarely calls for immediate reactions; indeed, the contrary is rather the case. Authority entails a presence that goes beyond mere control; it requires sustained attention. As the parent of an infant or toddler, you need eyes in the back of your head. Danger is everywhere: the stairs, the stove, even kitchen utensils. As children get older, the dangers become more complex: roads, friends, the internet. This is the place for parentalism (not paternalism). Parents want to take care of their children, and that's why they decide what is good for them and what isn't. If their decisions don't conform to convention, they are corrected from within the community. Or in Omer's view: from within the collective.

Vigilant care based on presence — that sounds all well and good. But when parents increase their presence, they are very soon confronted with things they would rather not have known (their 13-year-old daughter standing on street corners, smoking). Pretending not to see, or sheepishly making excuses, is not a good idea. Head-on confrontation leads to an escalation and ends up simply displacing the problem (their daughter now smokes in places where they won't see her). So what is the right course of action? This example demonstrates the difference between pure power and authority. Power demands obedience, and that obedience must be immediate ('Give me those cigarettes!'), which means that there always must be a winner and a loser. It's not a foregone conclusion that the parent is always the winner ('Hey, I bought them with my own money!'). Accusations lead to defensive behaviour and denial, which do little to help reach a solution. Severe punishments even less so. Pure power fails because it demands unconditional obedience.

Authority focuses on future voluntary submission, which is far less bound to one person. A parent can make it clear that smoking is anything but a good idea, that he or she will talk to the other parent and with a few further key people about it, and return to the issue later (after talking to the others). All these statements communicate a message of care and concern. The fact that the teenager won't understand this until (much) later is not a problem. Vigilant care has lasting authority as its aim, which is diametrically opposed to immediate action. And indeed, it's about communicating statements, not about issues that are up for discussion (smoking *is* very bad for you, period). As Hannah Arendt says: authority does not work through the medium of persuasion.

This is the way a collective works, in consultation with others — asking what other parents think about the problem (what time should a 15-year-old be expected to come home from a party?). Some parents will have to change their opinions, others will see their views vindicated, and, in both cases, authority has its basis in a group — a basis that's communicated as such to the teenager ('I phoned your classmates' parents, and they told me …').

In this approach, the question is no longer whether a teacher or parent 'has' enough authority as an individual. No single parent or teacher can command authority on his or her own. Anyone who has 'authority' on their own in fact has only power. A remarkable feature of Omer's approach is that it means appealing to those next to us, not to someone who towers above us (such as the headmaster). The new authority rests upon a network, which immediately offers more opportunity to guarantee the necessary presence. Moreover, this network also includes the teenager's peers; the social control and pressure exerted by the peer group are immense. The size of the network dictates another condition: transparency.

Sharing with the group — the benefits of transparency

When parents have a problem with their children, they often tend to want to deal with it behind closed doors. But concealing something in this way has all sorts of unwanted consequences. The scale of the unspeakable thing increases exponentially, as does the associated social isolation. The parent is then in the weakest position, and the young person becomes the powerful one. In extreme cases, this can even lead to blackmail ('What if Grandma finds out about … ?').

Parents — especially single mothers — often feel they're being blamed, sent to stand in the corner, as it were, and this only serves to increase their isolation. No wonder they conceal things and are reluctant to cooperate with care workers. Hence the justified appeal from child psychiatrist Myriam Maes: parents of children with problems always feel like failures, so, teachers and care workers, please don't make them feel even more guilty. Bring them out of isolation; see parents as partners, not as culprits. They are partners within a network.

Ideally, it will be the parents themselves who bring the problem out into the open — preferably as soon as possible — with the aim of finding a common position. If a party in their teenage son's bedroom degenerates into an orgy of binge drinking, the best course of action is to contact the parents of the other revellers, rather than avoiding them. Secrecy will never last long in today's world, anyway (there's a considerable chance that sonny boy will have posted a set of extremely embarrassing photos on Facebook during the drinking session).

Transparency surrounding problems that used to be dealt with behind closed doors evokes a certain feeling: shame, which Lacan identifies as the emotion that best suits the person in the dominant position. Yet however embarrassing it is, shame is preferable to guilt. Guilt implies punishment and often leads to exclusion (scapegoating). Shame opens up possibilities for rectification, in which the shamed party can take an active role. Omer places a clear focus in this context: avoid punishment, aim for rectification, and — most importantly — allow the young person to join in with considerations of how he or she can best cooperate.

As a reminder: the two factors that determine the success of psychotherapeutic treatment are the relationship between the client and the care worker, and the extent to which the client can make an active contribution to his or her own recovery. This participation should also ideally take place in a transparent manner, so that the client's recovery is recognised in the broader group.

Authority in place of power

Authority which appeals to and is founded on a horizontal network is radically different from the pyramidal version in which a patriarch rules from the top down. The latter model no longer works; those who want to occupy an alpha position stand alone, and instead of loyal underlings, they mainly encounter competitors, opportunists, and hangers-on within their own ranks.

Such a solitary position is just what Omer wants to avoid. In a confrontation with a student, a teacher no longer has to ask which of them can be the boss, but how to appeal to others: 'What help can I expect from my colleagues?' Note: from my colleagues, not from my headmaster.

In transitioning to a collective authority, a certain threshold must be crossed: this approach doesn't allow for avoiding confrontation. We have become increasingly afraid of confrontation, certainly in parenting and education. The disappearance of traditional authority means that such confrontations almost always descend into power struggles. And then there can only ever be losers, who will then be bent on revenge, and so it can only be a matter of time before the next confrontation blows up. That changes in a collective authority. An adult does not have to 'win' a confrontation, and the young person is also not the 'loser'. Success doesn't depend on agreement (viz. submission) from the youngster, but it does depend on the constancy of the adult, combined with a knowledge that he or she is sufficiently supported by the group.

Restoring authority means restoring security. As a result, children and teenagers who have sided with a bully, for example, will also become part of the group. Before, they felt compelled to be loyal to the bully, partly out of fear, and partly out of a desire to be among the 'winners'; as soon as that pattern is broken, those feelings disappear. Adult alpha-bullies also have a group of so-called loyal followers, whose loyalty vanishes when the alpha male falls from his pedestal.*

In the context of parenting, the most important

---

* In her book *Alles over pesten* (*All about Bullying*), Mieke van Stigt describes the possible effects a peer group can have, ranging from radical exclusion and social control to support. All cases show the power of a group dynamic, including among children and teenagers. Bullying is about power and the distribution of power positions in a context where there's little or no authority. In my view, the disappearance of classic authority and the descent into pure power provide an important explanation for today's all-pervading culture of bullying. Introducing a horizontal system of authority is the most effective response to this.

difference between power and authority is that power demands complete obedience, while authority permits autonomy. Since autonomy is the eventual aim of parenting and education, the earlier it starts, the better. In the approach proposed by Omer, for example, it's brought about by asking teenagers to come up with solutions themselves for the problems they have caused (rather than facing punishment) — solutions that allow them to repair the damage they've caused. This reparation allows them to rebuild confidence in themselves and others.

Limiting this approach to individual psychological treatments would send the wrong signal: teachers/parents can't cope with the situation, they have too little authority; the problem is the child, who has a disorder. The proper place for the psychologist is within the school, within the community, as part of the collective, and not outside of it — for example to guide the group from within as it transitions to shared authority, all in the style of this new form of authority.

This approach needn't be imposed 'from above' — on the contrary. Such an idea belongs to the classic model, in which people hope that 'the top' will come up with solutions, only to see these solutions fail. For the new method to be introduced, all it requires is for a couple of people to take the initiative together — the chances that others will follow are very high. In doing this, they will immediately contribute to restoring what our age so desperately needs: social connectedness.

Parenting, education, and authority

For obvious reasons, parenting and education create the foundations of the way in which a person deals with authority. Parenting and education determine our identity, and authority is one of the four central relations from which identity is formed. Thus, social changes regarding authority become apparent in parenting and education first.

This evolution is now fully underway, moving towards the group, and coming — as is so often the case — from below. I am thinking of small-scale initiatives where parents take turns to provide before- and after-school care for their children. Without even realising it, they're creating a collective authority. One step further, and they will do this consciously, including the school in their arrangements, for example. Their experience will also have consequences in other areas of life.* The move from sharing childcare duties and carpooling to group purchasing energy isn't so big, and takes this approach into another sphere — our economic activities.

The word economy comes from the Greek *oikos*, house, and in its narrowest sense it means 'housekeeping'. So, what kind of authority is at work in our *oikonomia*?

---

* Here's one example with an immediate political significance: a group of parents in Amsterdam has taken the initiative to make their children's school, the Visserschool, less ethnically segregated.

SEVEN
YOUR MONEY OR
YOUR LIFE

The Israeli historian Yuval Harari is a gifted storyteller who takes his readers on a more-than-400-page journey through the history of *Sapiens* — that is, our own species. More than 400 pages, and the reader is still sorry to reach the end of Harari's book of that name. One of the astonishing insights Harari offers is about money. What does it mean? How does it work? In a nutshell: it means nothing — unless you believe in it. Originally, we believed that a silver or gold coin contained a standard amount of the corresponding precious metal; later, we believed a banknote could be exchanged for gold, since every national bank maintained the necessary gold reserves (the so-called gold standard ended in 1971). Nowadays, the question is whether we believe that banks, countries, and institutions are able to pay their debts.

The parallel with authority is obvious. Just like authority, the power of money rests on the belief in an external basis. This used to be a tangible guarantee, namely national gold reserves; now it's based on creditworthiness. For those who

still have a few scraps of Latin: credit comes from *credo* —
'I believe (that you will pay me back)'. Thus, faith in money
rests on faith alone; there's no other external basis. If you
prick it, the entire bubble bursts. The hot air of the virtual
economy has come to smell pretty burnt.*

The aspect of 'faith' isn't restricted to money, but affects
the entire free-market economy. A hundred years ago,
Weber identified the roots of capitalism in Protestantism,
and many authors since have elaborated on that theory.
We think that we've left religion behind us, but today's
capitalism is the secular version of Christianity — an even
more coercive version, if that's possible. Everything is based
on debt, but the chance of redemption has gone. The system
is such that the debt can never be paid off, and is therefore
passed on to the next generation (like original sin). This is
true not only for individuals, but also for countries, whose
state of grace is periodically judged by special institutions
of the capitalist church (rating agencies) (highest score
AAA). And heaven is, of course, a tax haven.[1]

Viewed from a distance, our economic system is a
strange thing. A literary device commonly used by writers
during the Enlightenment to expose the absurdities of the
society of their time was to introduce a foreign character —

---

* By 'virtual economy', I mean the trade in so-called 'financial
products', which is trading in debts. This is far removed from the
real economy, in which goods and services are produced. Nowadays,
the virtual economy is far more important than the real one, and
many economists are convinced that it's helping to kill off the real
economy ('Wall Street is killing Main Street').

preferably a cultivated person from an exotic land — who described wide-eyed what he saw in his host country. In our times, such a foreigner might say: 'Imagine a country where almost no one makes anything real anymore, no, really, almost nobody. They leave that to slaves in other countries. The only thing they create themselves, that they *have* to create themselves, is debt, all of them. And that's only the beginning! You won't believe it, but those debts are bought by other people, in businesses set up especially for that purpose. The purchasers do something with them that they call "repackaging". This actually means that they lump together different debts to form new "products" — yes, really, they call them "products" — which they can then sell on to yet others. To keep everything running, people in that country are always taking out loans with one another, more and more loans. They call that "growth". Every now and then, they talk about cutbacks, but only for the lowest levels of society.'

What the noble foreigner doesn't realise is that no one still believes in this religion of credit — yet nobody dares be the first to abandon it.

The system is in power

For quite some time now, neoliberal capitalism has been a self-perpetuating system, partly because Margaret Thatcher's credo — 'there is no alternative' — is still hammered home by our current politicians, and partly because, as the dominant system, neoliberal capitalism manages to neutralise any threat perfectly by absorbing it. The revolutionary values of the 1968 student protests (authenticity, creativity, autonomy …) were long ago coopted as the virtues of the 'free' market. A movie like *Wall Street*, which should have served as an indictment, instead gave young people something to identify with: 'Greed is good. Greed is right. Greed works.'[2]

Providing state guarantees or — for goodness' sake — nationalising a bank means that a country is supporting the system. The only question is whether a guaranteed basic income ('free money', as it was described by the Dutch historian Rutger Bregman) won't soon become another neoliberal promotional stunt. People must keep on buying. If they can't get any more credit, shouldn't we just give them the money?[3] Moreover, this already happens, albeit not at the level of the individual. 'Free money' is the way I see the decision of the European Central Bank in 2015 to print an extra trillion euros with the aim of stimulating 'growth'.

Tinkering with details — even if it appears revolutionary — doesn't have the desired effect on the system; often, the opposite is true. The solution doesn't lie in curtailing bonuses, sacking haughty CEOs, removing socialists from governments, or 'attacking' the headquarters of multinational corporations. The only thing that will help is a fundamental change, a radical overhaul of the system itself. That *is* an alternative.

This radical change won't come out of nowhere. A conviction that's shared by increasing numbers of people — that this economic system has a built-in error — often leads to the idea that we need not do anything: the system is bound to collapse of its own accord. But the facts tell a different story: the successive crises it's been through have simply served to strengthen and toughen the system. Again and again, the solution to these crises has been to take even more neoliberal measures. When a nation-state takes over a bank, the nation-state itself soon begins operating as a business, and is given a rating from such agencies as Standard & Poor's — as in, poor may well become the new standard — raising the possibility of the country declaring bankruptcy.

Credit-rating agencies became necessary when companies began operating on the basis of substantial loans: is a given company able to pay off those loans? From the moment that the gold standard for national currencies was abandoned, the agencies began rating countries — is a given country able to honour its debts? The problem with this is that these credit-rating agencies are part of the system themselves, and sell advice both to those taking the loans and those giving them. And that means they've forfeited their integrity.[4]

We are ruled by a power that no authority can apparently match. We — meaning politicians, citizens, employers, and employees. Virtually everyone feels dissatisfied with today's economy, but no one seems able to change it. This is the most convincing evidence that a change must come about. And such a transformation must be supported by a new kind of authority.

Before we examine that, we should take a look at how and why this system maintains itself. The key word here is 'growth'.

But I can't keep on growing forever!

No growth — no jobs! No growth — no social security! These are two mantras of the new religion. These concepts have now become so generally accepted that no one dares question them. No one, that is, except my secretary, who said at her umpteenth yearly assessment, 'But I can't keep on growing forever!' In this, she proved George Orwell was right when he said (in 1945) something like, 'There are some ideas that are so absurd only an intellectual would believe them. Ordinary people would not be that stupid'. Let's examine those mantras a little more closely.

First and foremost: all the hysteria about growth tends to obscure the fact that economies *are* still growing. The fear is that they are growing too slowly, and, most importantly, less than predicted. So there's solid growth, but it's not enough. This leads any person in their right mind to ask, 'Enough to increase employment and guarantee social security?' But, no, despite this growth, jobs are disappearing quickly and the welfare state is being dismantled bit by bit.

In Western Europe, unemployment continues to increase, as do the attempts of virtually all governments to make the statistics appear a good deal rosier than they really are. This explains why the media sometimes speak of the 'official jobless figures' and the 'real number of people out of work'.[5] According to Robert Gordon, an American expert in unemployment, 45 per cent of middle class jobs will be lost over the next decade, through outsourcing and automation. What he fails to mention is that this rise in the number of jobless constitutes progress for our kind of economy. People are either consumers or (human) resources and are therefore a cost factor, a wage bill. As a cost factor, they must be quantified and contained. What does an unemployed person, a disabled person, a pensioner cost? Whatever the answer, it's always too much. And how much does an average employee cost? Preferably as little as possible. Oh, and not to forget: how much does a child cost?

Words are never innocent. If people are a 'cost factor', then as much saving as possible must be made with them. So outsource jobs to countries where child labour and wage slavery are still allowed, and replace people with machines. Make education and care as expensive as possible, or even better: turn them into profitable businesses. Prisons and old people's homes (note the combination!) have become a very interesting investment prospect: they're always full, inmates have little say, and there are no worries about customer loyalty — in one, they will never be coming back; in the other, they have no choice. Here, too, companies can skimp on the cost factor of 'human resources' by expressing work in terms of the number of minutes each old person is allocated for showering, for example. In Germany, the average care time for an old person has been whittled down to 50 minutes a day. Outsourcing has now also become an option. It's more profitable to set up a care home for elderly Germans in Eastern Europe — and why shouldn't we turn inmates into an export product?[6]

The mantra 'no growth — no jobs' is not true. Our modern economy grows and continues to grow, while requiring ever-fewer workers. An ironic example: in 2014, the banks laid off chiefly those employees who had created the most profits. The reason? Computer software could carry out their work faster and more efficiently.

And it has become painfully clear that the mantra 'no growth — no social security' is also untrue. A few years ago, practically every newspaper in my country ran the same headline in its New Year's edition: 'the stock market grew by 12 per cent this year'. Inside the paper, there were articles on how much the planned government cuts would cost the average citizen in 2015, and how the social-security system would be jeopardised. There were also articles about how the appallingly low rate of tax on company profits is completely legal, thanks to those smart Luxembourgers, as LuxLeaks taught us. If we take all those reports together, we see that, despite the growth and the profits on the stock market, social security was to be the main victim of the cuts.

This is no coincidence. This kind of economy can only benefit from increased insecurity and unstable employment. Hence the success of temporary-employment agencies. The International Labour Organisation publishes a yearly report on the development of labour around the world. The 2015 edition of the *World Employment and Social Outlook* says that job insecurity is increasing everywhere because full-time, permanent work contracts are on the decline around the world.[7] What's the best way to deal with the most significant cost factor (human beings)? Keep them insecure and afraid.

Here's a prediction, just on the side. Despite the powerful economic argument in favour of a guaranteed basic income (there has to be consumers), it may be rejected by those invested in 'the system'. Not because a basic income is unaffordable (as usual, the calculations vary, but the Swiss believe it is at least feasible. Their trains run on time, so I have confidence in their abilities with numbers), but because a basic income provides stability, and this makes people far more difficult to manipulate, and thus less susceptible to power.

Virtual growth and real debts

Today's growth, then, does not increase employment and certainly doesn't maintain social security. So what is it good for? And why does there always have to be *more* of it? And why is there panic when growth figures turn out to be lower than hoped? The answer is pretty absurd: the economy has to grow in order to be able to pay off the debts it has taken on in order to be able to grow ...

In today's economic system, growth is no longer based on an increase in *real* production (remember our exotic visitor). Real growth is based on innovation, and innovation is usually based on basic research carried out by scientific institutions. Forget the myth of the lone genius developing a fantastic idea in his garage, completely independently, only then to encounter resistance from the government when he tries to realise his idea. Innovation economist Mariana Mazzucato describes the way 12 technologies (from the internet to touchscreens) grew out of government-funded basic research. Nowadays, funding for such research has all-but disappeared and the money is being pumped into applied research. 'Applied' means: immediately profitable. In practice, this means, at best, improved versions of pre-existing technologies, not innovations.

No innovation, no real growth. What's called growth is mainly based on 'creative' interventions on financial 'markets'.[8] These are based on credit and therefore on debt and on the increase in debt trading. Virtual profits generated by virtual work feed virtual growth based on real debts, which sooner or later will have to be paid by real people. 'Too little growth' causes panic among our policy leaders not just, or not principally, because it means they will be able to pay off fewer debts, but because they'll have to take on more debts.

In this way, 'growth' and debt have each other locked in a deadly stranglehold. In order to 'grow', the economy has to take on a lot of debt. In order to pay off that debt, the economy has to grow more, and therefore take on even more debt. Since March 2015, the European Central Bank (ECB) has been pumping billions of euros into the European economy. The way this is being done and the underlying intention would make our exotic onlooker seriously doubt our mental capacities. The ECB is simply printing euros (after all, money is nothing but an agreement, an IOU) in order ... to buy up the national debt of some countries. The intention is to make banks in those countries more willing to offer loans (more debt) as a way of stimulating the growth of their economies.*

---

* The expectation is that this action will cause people with savings (people without debts, shame on them!) to lose money (interest

This whole argument is so absurd and so incredible that I find it necessary to reiterate it: money is simply being printed in order to buy debt so that more debts can be made. And that will lead to growth. Completely aside: sooner or later, those new debts will also have to be paid off, and the 'agreement' is that they will be paid off by taxpayers (that is, you and me).

Today's economy operates in a very virtual world, so it's high time for a reality check. If growth in the real world eventually comes down to an increase in CO_2 emissions, squandering of resources, and environmental degradation, then arguing for more growth is a crime against humanity. The economy of the future must be sustainable or it will not survive. It's as simple as that.

Your money or your life!

When I played 'cops and robbers' as a child, I didn't understand the dilemma inherent in the demand 'Your money or your life!' Whichever you choose, you're done for. Now, we are all facing this dilemma. Many people — including, or perhaps especially, politicians — realise this, but feel both powerless and fearful. The system is stronger

---

on their savings falls to zero, or even into negative territory), and they will then 'come to their senses' and start living on credit, too. Households now follow the same logic: 'grow' on the basis of debts. According to figures released by the National Bank of Belgium, the level of indebtedness at the start of 2014 was twice as high as it was ten years earlier, having risen to €217 billion (Du Caju, 2014).

than them, and the first person to put their head above the parapet will be shot down; that's the fear. However, the case of Iceland paints a very different picture. When the credit bubble burst, the country's economy was among the first to collapse. But the solution it chose is completely different to what happened, and is still happening, elsewhere in Europe. Let's look at what the Icelanders did.

The Icelandic government allowed the biggest banks to fail, and put them into receivership at the end of 2008. The country uncoupled its currency from the euro in order to devalue it. A new bank was set up for the Icelanders, which rescued their savings. The people forced the government to resign in early 2009. The new government distributed the burden of the collapse fairly, punished criminal activities in the Icelandic financial world, and quickly imposed drastic reforms on its national bank, which are still being implemented today. Following a referendum, the government refused to pay back lost investments, mostly from Dutch and British savers, using the money of Icelandic savers. In writing a new constitution, the Icelandic government turned to deliberative democracy (more on this in the next chapter).[9] In March 2012, Iceland paid back the last of the rescue loans it took from the International Monetary Fund. What we see here is a system change, expressly supported by the collective as a new form of authority, and going against the old power.

Iceland is a nice example, but what can we do as individual Europeans? Politics is ruled by economic interests that even the European Union can barely deal with, let alone a state. As individuals, we feel completely powerless, although we have a powerful weapon in our hands. The merging of politics and economics gives us, as consumers, more influence than we think, as is powerfully summed up in the expression 'When you are buying, you are voting'. Our consumer behaviour can be very influential, if we have the right information. I no longer buy books from Amazon, now that I know how they treat their workers; I don't fly with the Ryanairs of this world, for the same reason; and an investigative report in the newspaper made me decide not to pave my driveway with Kandla Grey sandstone, because it's quarried using child labour.

My reactions are part of a process that's now become typical: newspapers and broadcasters publish reports about the misconduct of a multinational company, prompting people to start a protest campaign on social media. This is how Starbucks was forced to pay tax in the United Kingdom, after a boycott by their customers.

Our awareness of this power that we hold is growing as our knowledge of the malpractices in companies' production methods and personnel policies also increases. Social control is not limited to the people in our immediate environment, but also applies to businesses. They have now discovered that ethical policies can be a powerful advertising tool. Supermarkets sell Fairtrade products (which is incidentally a Dutch initiative, having begun with the Max Havelaar coffee label). Timber traders can flaunt a seal from the Forest Stewardship Council, proving that they cooperate with ecologically sound forestry companies. The same is true of sea fishing, with its Marine Stewardship

Council label, which certifies sustainable fishing. Many major supermarket chains now sell only fish that bears the MSC label.* Initiatives such as these are often the result of collaboration between industry, environmental organisations, and various civil-society groups. Traditional politics is rarely involved.[10]

It's worth noting that this is all about *real* products in the *real* economy. A similar approach to the virtual economy barely exists, but it is gradually growing, with the Dutch Triodos Bank as a shining example of ethical banking. In 2009, the *Financial Times* named Triodos as the most sustainable bank. Many small-scale initiatives are springing up, such as the financial-services provider Hefboom, which works exclusively with ethical and sustainable projects.

Such changes grow out of decisions at the management level. Nowadays, economic activity is a management issue. If there is to be a new kind of authority within economics, there must be a new management culture.

---

* The information about the FSC and the MSC comes from Jared Diamond's book *Collapse*. Diamond investigates why certain historical cultures went under. His conclusion is both frightening and hopeful: the main reasons for a collective collapse of a society boil down to, among other things, a combination of climate change and bad decisions: 'Throughout recorded history, actions or inactions by self-absorbed kings, chiefs, and politicians have been a regular cause of societal collapses'. The hopeful message is that some societies do make the right choices and do not collapse. There is an alternative, but it rarely, if ever, comes from a great leader. 'Chief among the forces affecting political folly is lust for power'.

There is an alternative, after all (1): horizontal management

'The heart of the problem is the pyramid, the basic organising principle of the modern corporation.' These are the words of Brazilian CEO Ricardo Semler, and he should know what he's talking about. At the start of his career, he restructured Semco, the company set up by his father, following the traditional American business model. And the company grew (12 levels of management!), and profits increased, to applause all round. Just five years later, Ricardo found himself in an unhealthy combination of *The Office* and *Game of Thrones*: careerists, struggles for status, deceit, treachery, overregulation, lack of motivation, stomach ulcers. He then spent another ten years introducing a horizontal organisation to the company. Semco is now a success in all possible areas.

Before I read Semler's book *Maverick!*, I was dubious. Management books written by self-styled gurus — not really my thing. After reading the book, I was so enthused that my enthusiasm made me quite suspicious once more. So I looked for a serious criticism of his model. But I found nothing convincing. If you are a manager who wants to set up a successful organisation, take inspiration from Semler. Of course, there is a 'but': you have to throw the entire classical business hierarchy out of the window, including your own position at the top of it.

Anyone who's now expecting an argument in favour of the classic left-wing approach will be disappointed, I'm afraid. Command and control were just as ingrained in the communist and socialist organisations of the previous century, and, at crucial moments, it was predominantly the trade unions who opposed Semler's reforms. Anyone expecting a detailed how-to guide on 'the' Semco model will be even more disappointed. How-to guides belong to the top-down approach, just like the organisational charts and protocols that are erroneously thought to be universally applicable. A Western European business model applied in Africa (everybody starts work at 8.30 a.m.) doesn't work; a Japanese model applied in an American shipyard (all singing together in the morning) doesn't work. Semco is rather a way of thinking based on a number of principles, any application of which will be different, but whose function is always the same. The basic idea is horizontality.

The good news is that it works, even in the long term. But the bad news is that it inevitably leads to job losses. Not at the bottom, as is usually the case with company restructuring, but at the top. Of the 12 original management levels at his company, Semler retained just three. This presumably explains why those in executive positions are not exactly falling over themselves to introduce this system.

It's risky to list the principles involved — a way of thinking can't easily be translated into well-defined principles. A list of key concepts is better — keys can be used to open rusty old locks and rescue sleeping princesses from high towers. Trust. Transparency. Self-organisation. Production cells. Consultation. Divide and grow.

Trust. In its original, American version, Semler's company had extensive systems in place to prevent theft by employees. Investigations showed him that only 3–5 per cent of his employees were potential thieves, but everyone was subject to the many control procedures, which cost a lot of money. Semler scrapped them, which itself led to substantial savings. He gradually realised something else: in a climate of trust, people won't tolerate cheats. After a certain time, social control took over and his employees began getting rid of untrustworthy colleagues themselves.

Transparency. Trust is greatly enhanced by transparency. In a pyramidal structure, each higher level 'knows' more than the one below, and each lower level distrusts the one above. Withholding knowledge bestows power, albeit usually imaginary power, and leads to wild interpretations among those who don't possess it. Semler has a policy of total transparency. All information is available to everyone (except for technical trade secrets). The most important kind of information is financial: who earns what, and what profits does the company make on what products or services. But also: what are the losses, what ideas are being considered to tackle them, and so on. Not only is all information available, but also employees may receive a short in-company training in how to read and understand it.

Self-organisation. The most important area in which there must be trust is the organisation of labour. People usually know very well how they can organise their work most efficiently, so they should be allowed to decide for themselves by mutual agreement. Semler has shown this applies equally to a pharmacy with seven employees or to a large company like Semco. Let the employees arrange their products themselves, for example, and the results will be (1) time savings, (2) more accurate orders and less stockpiling, (3) greater satisfaction among both the staff and the customers, and (4) more profits. The explanation is simple: employees often have more practical knowledge than someone just sitting in an office thinking about things. They should be trusted. The result is that they feel listened to and acknowledged, that they identify more with their work and take responsibility for it.

Production cells. Autonomous units consisting of a maximum of 150 people work exclusively on one product. Forget Charlie Chaplin's character in *Modern Times*, who has to perform the same action in the same position on the same machine over and over again. That's Taylorism, a scientifically developed and tested method for maximising productivity — with a maximum loss of motivation as the predictable side effect. When a team tasked with finishing a certain product as optimally as possible is left to self-organise, the result is a high degree of motivation and job satisfaction. And it renders any kind of 'quality care' mechanism obsolete, because such a team will ensure the quality of the product itself. This approach also includes a focus on task rotation. Employees are stimulated to acquire as many skills as they can, so they are easily able to take over a task from someone else in their production cell, can join in discussions about better ways to organise certain tasks, and quickly learn to complete new tasks. Great importance is given to mobility within the company.

Consultation. Self-organisation doesn't mean that people can just do as they please. Employees are in constant consultation with each other and, on the basis of those consultations, take decisions that are subject to social control. This is much more effective than rules imposed from above, which mainly serve to stoke discontent and collective resistance. If employees can't agree, they can request a consultation with one of the three levels of management (first-line management, business-unit management, and general management). The three levels are not arranged hierarchically, but also operate in consultation with each other. If you want to imagine how this works, picture three interwoven and intersecting circles (for those familiar with mathematical topology: Borromean rings).

Those who imagine endless meetings when they think of 'consultation' are wrong. Semler clearly has a visceral hatred of meetings, since they are restricted to two per week in his company, and they may not go on for longer than two hours. Everyone spends the rest of their working time (the working week minus four hours) … working, and any consultation that may be necessary between people takes place in the workplace.

Divide and grow. Trust, transparency, and self-organisation aren't possible if the group is too large. The members must be able to get to know each other personally, and exchanges must take place in the real world — digital contact is not enough. That's why the maximum size of a production cell is 150 people, and they're preferably smaller. The more-than-5000 employees at Semco work in completely autonomous units of that size, and even have their own company entrance, canteen, and so on. Proponents of upscaling will reject this as 'uneconomical', arguing that it negates all the benefits of large-scale operations (centralised and therefore cheaper infrastructure, bulk buying and therefore better prices, etc.). Semler illustrates what many people have experienced themselves in this time of constant company mergers and centralisation: a smaller organisation functions much more efficiently and economically — the bigger the organisation, the greater the wastage.

The company has more unorthodox rules. For example, production teams are involved in decisions about hiring new staff members, even for management positions. Evaluations go both ways and can have far-reaching effects, even to the point of dismissals. Employees can decide what proportion of real profits goes to the staff and how it should be distributed. Working from home is actively encouraged.

Let me just repeat: this company is profitable and — judging by such things as absenteeism due to sickness, strikes, and job-application figures — is a particularly pleasant place to work.[11]

The authority of the group

Semco operates with an entirely different form of authority than traditional organisations. In the glossary at the back of Semler's book, the following is the entry for 'paternalism':

> A dirty word at Semco. We don't want to be one
> big happy family. We want to be a successful
> company. We are concerned only with the

work performance of our people, not with their personal lives. You won't find a running track, swimming pool or gym at Semco ... Rather than treating our employees like children who need to be looked after all the time, we treat them like adults who are perfectly capable of making their own decisions.

Semler finds the basis for his kind of authority in the same entity as the new parenting model of Haim Omer: the collective. In this case, that means a group of people who carry out tasks in mutual consultation, at a company that they want to keep as sustainable as possible.

The key question then becomes: how does horizontal authority work? Does a spontaneous self-organisation appear horizontally in and between groups of small size? I suspect that some readers will be harbouring this illusion. Get rid of managers, get rid of hierarchy, and trust in the goodness of humankind. This conjures up lovely images of little village communities living together in harmony, both with each other and with nature. Yet anthropological studies have shown that one of the main causes of death in such communities is violence.[12] Belief in spontaneous self-organisation is a dangerous illusion, comparable with the delusional idea of self-regulation in the ideology of the free market, the 'invisible hand'. A horizontal organisation can only work within certain limits. It took Semler ten years to learn what those limits are.

We don't need to find out those limits for ourselves. They have existed for a long time, and go back to the idea of the commons (commonly owned land or property), an economic phenomenon that has been reinterpreted since the advent of the internet. Until the 18th century, large stretches of land were used collectively by a community to graze their livestock, to chop firewood, or dig peat, or so on. Hence the word 'commons', as the property was there for the common good. Over roughly half a century, the upper class seized the common land and fenced it off — the only exception in Europe is Switzerland, where the system is still in place.

To this day, the prevailing belief is that collective use of a commons is not a good idea. This goes back to an essay written by Garrett Hardin in 1968 called 'The Tragedy of the Commons'. This American ecologist had little faith in human nature and assumed that everyone must be out to profit as much as he or she can from such a common resource. His proposed solution was central management along the lines of a 'command and control' model. Forty years later, the empirical studies of the Nobel Prize–winning economist Elinor Ostrom proved precisely the opposite. But even today, the unsubstantiated opinions of Hardin are held up as an argument against the commons model, while Ostrom's work goes largely ignored. Recent research shows that 'free enterprise' often leads to overexploitation, while common ownership often leads to sustainability. Local fishermen will not overfish their waters, but can only stand by and watch as giant trawlers deplete their fish stocks.[13]

There is an alternative, after all (2): commons

The idea that commons are a kind of anarchist hippie commune with no rules, where everyone casually shares everything (and everyone sleeps with everyone) is a great misconception. Elinor Ostrom describes a number of features — in fact, requirements — that she recognises in almost all commons.

Before we examine them, it's more than worth pointing out two characteristics that commons share with both the Semco model and the new parenting model of Haim Omer. The first is that participants maintain close contact with each other in the reality of everyday life. Omer, too, points out that presence is a prerequisite for parenting. Social control can never be replaced by digital control, and horizontal authority requires real interaction.

The second shared feature is that there's no guidebook, no protocol for setting up the perfect commons. In fact, the opposite is true: Ostrom's research shows that applying such a 'one size fits all' model (often imposed on local economies by governments or multinationals) almost always has disastrous effects. What she did see were five recurring constraints.

First, a common good must be shared by a clearly defined group. Not just anybody can come along, make use of the common good, and go away again.

Second, use of the common good occurs according to rules that, in the case of a traditional piece of common agricultural land, for example, determine when and how much can be harvested. These rules will have existed for a long time, even having grown organically within the group, and are suited to the local situation.

This explains the third constraint: the group can change the rules in mutual agreement, and this indeed happens regularly. That makes commons flexible organisations, able to react rapidly to changing conditions.

The fourth constraint is all-pervading social control. All other members of the group monitor closely how individuals treat the common property.

And that leads to the fifth constraint. Every commons has a way of punishing rule breakers. In her study, Ostrom notes that the punishments are relatively light and applied only quite rarely. The most important sanction is in fact much less tangible: those who break the rules lose their reputation, and, within a community, that's the worst thing that can happen to someone.

Ostrom's research reveals a very striking observation. When people are able and allowed to decide on their own individual wellbeing in the context of common interests, they consistently opt for long-term solutions that serve the common good.[14]

Commons and cooperatives: the sharing economy

Many people will nod understandingly when they hear reports about the commons and cooperative companies, all the while thinking that a multinational could never be run on a cooperative basis, and that commons models apply mainly to fishing and animal husbandry. To put it bluntly: they imagine it's just for tree-huggers.

Semco in Brazil is a counterexample, as an original combination of the commons and cooperative models. An example from the Netherlands is Buurtzorg Neighbourhood Nursing, set up by a man who was fed up with his job as a community nurse with an impersonal, centrally managed healthcare organisation. Buurtzorg now employs 8000 people, in more than 550 self-managed teams. It's more successful than any other healthcare company in the Netherlands, works for half the price, and was voted best Dutch employer for two successive years. Another example is Mondragon, the tenth-largest company in Spain (70,000 employees, more than 250 branches), which is run in a completely cooperative way. An example from Belgium shows how this can also work in the retail sector: a new approach that puts employees in a central position has led to Schoenen Torfs being voted employer of the year five times, and the shoe retail chain has also doubled its profits. The director of the Belgian Federal Public Service Social Security agency, Frank Van Massenhove, showed that a similar approach can succeed in the public sector. His motto is 'take back control of your own life'. In 2007, he was voted government manager of the year, and his department is one of the most popular employers within the Belgian civil service.[15]

Of course, it's not all moonlight and roses, and proponents of top-down models criticise it wherever they can. The reason for their opposition is, I think, very simple: it would mean them relinquishing their power. Whatever their reason for resisting, it cannot be based on economic motives. Compared to 'command and control' organisations, these companies do very well in terms of sustainability, profitability, and job creation. There certainly is an alternative, and it's gaining more and more ground.

In the last decade, the economy has increasingly reached beyond the traditional world of business. The combination of new means of communication via the internet and old forms of cooperation (commons/cooperatives) could well form the basis for a different kind of economy than the one we have today. How often do you use your electric drill? Less than half an hour a year. What about your hedge trimmer? Less than one day a year. These and other examples clearly show how uneconomical our current consumption habits are (except for the producers of those goods), and how beneficial sharing is.[16] Of course, there are some freeloaders, but the constraints discovered by Ostrom will kick in with time. Virtual communication allows people to share real things. And avoid getting into real debt.

Moreover, this kind of sharing goes far beyond just electric drills. One of the fastest growing commons/cooperatives is in the area of energy, where the focus lies on renewable energy sources (solar panels, wind-power generators). Commons/cooperatives almost always opt for sustainable solutions. Germany is once again a frontrunner, with a third of its energy already coming from renewable sources, but things are developing fast elsewhere.

This is all summed up by the phrase 'the sharing economy'. The concept of 'economic' is replaced here by that of 'economical', with the focus on 'thrift' rather than so-called 'growth'. When people are asked why they participate in such initiatives, the answers they give are obvious: it saves you a lot of money; it's better for the environment; it's easy and reliable; it gives you a sense of control over your consumption; it gives you the feeling of being part of a movement; and you meet new people.

The most important commodity we all share, once again thanks to digital technology, is knowledge. Michel Serres (*Thumbelina*) and Alessandro Baricco (*The Barbarians*) described this beautifully: knowledge is becoming a public commodity. There's Wikipedia, and there's more and more open-source software. Nerds are no longer just nerdy, they are the co-creators of programs that are mostly available for free on the net, from operating systems like Linux to Wikispeed, a modular-car design company. This no longer has a local character, since the internet knows no borders. The new social space is glocal, a portmanteau word combining global and local. Knowledge offers the basis for the new authority of the collective. Its social control also impacts on the business world. Companies that produce misleading advertising are roundly criticised on social media; businesses that deliver bad products or services soon feel the wrath of consumers on review websites.[17] The argument that these review sites are open to manipulation is principally an argument *against* the advertising industry, which has raised deception to the level of a science.

All these new initiatives have now created a new collective authority, which is, for the most part, based on the same principles as those outlined by Semler and Ostrom. The community is paramount, real interactions are necessary, information is exchanged as much as possible, mechanisms for control and sanctions exist, people can make their own decisions, and self-organisation and consultation are central. The basis for this collective authority is social trust and the associated social control. This leads to the kind of voluntary submission that is typical of authority, in combination with an almost automatic severity towards cheaters. The punishment they face is the same as it has been for centuries: exclusion.

The social and environmental significance of the sharing economy illustrates the difference to our current economy: from individual ownership to sharing and exchange, from growth to sustainability.

Sustainable economy or doom

If we are to have a future at all, it must be a sustainable one. Growth is no longer the solution, but the problem. Until roughly 50 years ago, when our economy was still a real rather than virtual one, *real* growth was an engine of social mobility, and an (almost) free market offered one of the best worlds imaginable. The free market at that time was explicitly linked to democracy, in contrast to the centrally planned state economies of the communist Eastern Bloc. The link between the free market and democracy has now been broken (the market is dictated by financial power monopolies); 'growth' is mostly virtual and benefits an ever-smaller minority. The solution of yesteryear is suicide today. More and more economists are beginning to understand this — but *The Herald of Free Enterprise* continues to sail on with its bow door open.*

Along with the free market, democracy is also disappearing. Already there are opinion makers who advocate for a reduction in democracy because it disrupts 'the market' too much.** The upward social mobility of the past now goes in the opposite direction, and increasing

---

* On 6 March 1987, the ferry *The Herald of Free Enterprise* sank almost immediately after leaving the Belgian port of Zeebrugge, drowning 193 people. The bow doors were still open when the ship set sail, and the ship's design included no watertight compartments on the car deck. Investigations placed the broad blame for the disaster on competitive pressure, which led to shortcomings in safety. From that perspective, the ship's name seems tragically ironic.

** John Micklethwait and Adrian Wooldridge describe this as 'the fourth revolution' in their book of that name. They argue implicitly for handing over political control to technocrats, who would principally be responsible for taking monetary and fiscal measures, over the heads of democratically elected governments. When two American writers hold up Singapore and China as model states, then the proverbial has really hit the fan. Their book is a typical example of manipulative rhetoric: evidence is cited very selectively (the information they give about Scandinavia is both false and incomplete), readers are tempted by an offer they are hardly likely to refuse (less waste, combatting tax evasion, better control of politicians), and, almost imperceptibly, readers are also fed a medicine that deprives them of their right to decide. One quote: 'But the West also runs the biggest risk: Listening to people is one reason why the West has become so overloaded …' Their ideal is clearly an anorexic state, 'efficiently' run by technocratic managers, with a minimum of influence from the citizens. Politicians who take this book as their guideline want to do away stealthily with democracy.

numbers of people are slipping down the social ladder. According to an OECD report from 2015, inequality is on the rise. And any sociological study will show that this leads to both an unhealthy and a dangerous society.

These economic issues have become completely political ones, if only because, until things change, politics is at the mercy of this type of economy. It long ago ceased to be about an opposition between the private sector and the government, in which 'government' stands for all that is bad and 'the private sector' represents all that is good. It's certainly no longer about 'streamlining' the government and 'freeing up' the market. The power of the government to control the needs of certain groups is in fact increasing, and the only thing that's being 'streamlined' is the work the government does to benefit society. The opposition today is between society on the one hand and financial monopolies on the other, while the latter have a stranglehold on governments and can force them to take decisions that aren't in the best interests of society — a society that politicians, as the people's elected representatives, are supposed to serve.

Let us put this to the test. Ostrom described the principles by means of which commons safeguard the interests of the community in the long term. As a thought experiment, we can turn those rules around, revealing the opposite principles, which go *against* the best interests of the community and which serve the interests of a small group in the short term. What are the results of such a thought experiment? What are the prerequisites for *Homo economicus* gaining the upper hand?

Firstly, no one is connected to a community any longer. You buy and sell shares at lightning speed without ever taking into account who or what those shares represent. A company can relocate you anywhere, so you move house again — no connection, no responsibility, no sustainability.

Secondly, make sure there are as few regulations as possible. Under the guise of 'freedom' and 'autonomy', you abolish them wherever you can. The more deregulation, the better. This creates all the more opportunities to go against the public interest and finally to ignore all that nonsense about the environment.

Thirdly, make sure that those who are still subject to the rules that do remain have no way of changing them, but that those who impose them from above can change them at will.

Fourthly, try to thwart transparency and social control as much as possible. 'What the eye doesn't see ...' Make sure everything happens behind closed doors.

Finally, impose hefty sanctions on anyone who opposes this drastic reduction to *Homo economicus*, and enforce complete obedience. Those who refuse to obey are told they are 'not accepting their responsibilities'.

Does any of that sound familiar? It's time to ask some political questions.

EIGHT

MR VALDEMAR
OR DELIBERATIVE
DEMOCRACY

For those who somehow haven't yet realised: traditional politics is over. Throughout Europe, membership of political parties is in freefall and turn-out for elections continues to plummet (even where voting is compulsory).[1] As I mentioned earlier, the father of the fatherland of times gone by now resembles the unwitting zombie Mr Valdemar. The popular contempt for politicians due to corruption and ineptitude finds its reflection in the condescension of some top politicians towards the electorate. In their view, voters are not only naive, but also indifferent, despite the fact that there's so much at stake.

And they are right in that. There is a lot at stake. But the first contention (that voters are indifferent and naive) is completely wrong — it's a long time since politics aroused so much interest. In the Dutch-speaking world alone, a dozen books were published last year dealing with democracy and, to judge by the number of reprints, they are finding an avid readership. In recent years, we've also seen a revival in protest movements, both in their traditional form, with demonstrations and strikes, and in their new incarnation: citizens who gather together and develop their own proposals for matters of public concern. In Germany, *Wutbürger*, 'enraged citizen', was voted word of the year for 2010.*

There's no longer any interest in traditional politics, except to express indignation at it. That includes protest voting, which explains the success of far-left and far-right politicians around the world. The failure of traditional politics has nothing to do with the popular view that there are no great statesmen anymore. The explanation goes far deeper than that, touching on the very structure of politics; the political pyramid has collapsed like a souffle because it no longer has any foundation. Our modern political system is in deep crisis.

Democracy and elections

Anyone who studies history from around the time of the Renaissance, with its popes and emperors and kings, to our age of parliamentary democracy cannot fail to see the link between politics and the patriarchy. Until recently, there was no place for women in traditional politics, which is overwhelmingly a place for strutting cockerels, where each

---

* Just a year later, the word was included in Germany's main reference dictionary, Duden, with the following definition: 'a citizen who is driven to vehement public protest and demonstrations by disappointment over certain political decisions'.

rooster demands ever-more power and always needs to crow on top of a higher dunghill than the next cock. The decline of the patriarchy means that there are no credible cockerels anymore, while we're still left to deal with piles of manure. Nowadays, no one believes in the existence of a super-cockerel. The lies of the likes of Blair, Chirac, and Berlusconi are still fresh in our memories.

The failure of the traditional political system has a dangerous side to it. Many people see it as the failure of democracy per se, and consequently as a legitimate reason to seek a different form of government. However, it is not 'democracy' that is failing. It's a certain interpretation of the democratic form of government that has become outdated, especially because that interpretation is no longer democratic at all. The search for an alternative to what is wrongly seen as a failed democracy could well lead to a totalitarian regime. Thus, to power instead of authority.

It's important to remind ourselves that our democracy is very young. Its origins may lie in the classical age, principally in fifth-century-BC Athens, but the nation-state didn't complete its gradual evolution into a parliamentary democracy until the early 19th century. That system is founded on elections, and has seen a tough struggle for universal suffrage. No wonder that we've come to see democracy almost as a synonym for free elections in which anybody can stand as a candidate and every vote has the same weight of influence.

How come, then, that voter turnout is on the decline everywhere?[2] I've already refuted the Mr Valdemar argument — that citizens are naive and indifferent. There is another explanation: voters are less and less willing to turn out for elections, or more and more likely to be floating voters, because they realise that their voices are not being heard. The once beautiful connection between elections and democracy is as good as gone. This surprising statement demands an explanation, and this is to be found in history. In a nutshell: initially, elections were not at all democratic; later, they were; and now, once again, they are not.

The first elections were deliberately aimed at restricting the power of the people as far as possible. The reason for that was explicitly paternalistic. Those in power considered the people to be stupid, and saw themselves as more competent to make decisions for those people. In that sense, the first elections were antidemocratic. Suffrage in Belgium was based on taxation, with only those above a certain tax threshold having the vote, and that amounted to a huge restriction in both the number of possible candidates and the number of voters. In both cases, these were men with money/status, and they made up less than 3 per cent of the total population.

The Netherlands introduced universal suffrage for adult males in 1917, and Belgium followed a year later, which was an enormous step forward for democracy. The extension of universal suffrage to women as well as men, in 1919 in the Netherlands but not until 1948 in Belgium, had an even greater impact on the spread of democracy. Practically every major social achievement dates from the decades that followed, and that's no coincidence. This was when governments were at their most democratic.

From 1980, we see politics giving way to economics. In

1966, President Charles de Gaulle was still able to claim that politics in France was not done at the stock exchange ('*La politique de la France ne se fait pas à la corbeille*'), but his successor took the country in a very different direction. From the 1980s on, classic authority gradually gave way to power, which was increasingly in the hands of financial and economic groups. Under the euphemistic term 'the free market', those groups still dominate politics, and therefore also governments, to this day, with the result that elections are no longer a guarantee of democracy. Just as it did in its earliest phase, the ballot box produces an aristocracy. Everyone senses this, but we are barely conscious of it. This recent development is so important that it requires further explanation.

A new aristocracy disguised as democracy

Aristocracy is a form of government in which a small elite holds the reins (the Greek word *aristoi* means 'the best'). The idea of the aristocracy conjures up images of ladies in rustling gowns, and counts and barons — that's the hereditary aristocracy, the nobility. Today, we're ruled by an electoral aristocracy that pretends to be democratic. This is all bound up with the evolution of political parties.

Initially, there were no parties, and the chosen delegates occupied their seats as independents. The first party in the Netherlands, the Anti-Revolutionary Party, was founded in 1879. The Liberal Union followed six years later, and the Social Democratic Party was established in 1894. Catholic politicians didn't come together in a party until 1926, when the General League of Roman Catholic Caucuses was formed. The reason for the development of different parties goes back to political and religious segregation in society. In Belgium, the first political party, the Liberal Party, was established in 1846. The first Catholic party dates from 1869, and the Belgian Labour Party followed in 1885. Looking at their origins, each of these parties was created in order to break, or at least weaken, a certain hegemony. The Liberal Party arose as a counterbalance to Catholic dominance. The Catholic party aimed originally to counter liberalism and later to make sure socialism was not the only option for workers looking for emancipation. The Belgian Labour Party was set up to oppose the parliamentary hegemony of the bourgeoisie. In essence, we see that political parties were created on an emancipatory footing. The development towards a rigid particracy — in which it is not the elected deputies but the party leaders and head offices that make policy decisions — came later.

Just as it was in the beginning, today, only a small group of people can de facto become candidates, due to financial, family, and intellectual demands. It's from among this already select group that party head offices draw their lists of candidates. So, which candidates make it onto the list, and which are given a safe seat to contest? The criteria are obscure and not always based on the number of votes won by individuals in previous elections. We see the same people cropping up every time we're called to the ballot box, and those figures eventually put forward their children as candidates, so that the electoral and hereditary aristocracy begin to merge. Many political parties have degenerated into family businesses, where the party is the battleground for two or three clans who are sworn enemies. Thus, our elections are antidemocratic right from the outset.

The elections themselves are less about content than about the media presence of individuals and their slogans ('Change now!'). In fact, the 'sacrament of democracy' has descended into a media spectacle directed by spin doctors recruited from the world of advertising. After the elections should come the period of government, but in practice it is rather a run-up to the next elections, in which the most important thing for politicians is that they must be seen to be scoring political points. This, too, is not conducive to a politics of substance rather than appearance.

To make matters worse, while they're in government office, our 'elected representatives of the people' take little or no account of what the people want. Practically every party that gets into government abandons its promises in no time, with a familiar platitude as their excuse: 'There is no alternative.' Furthermore, elected politicians do what their party headquarters tells them, which means that the country is governed in a top-down way by a tiny group of people. There's a yawning gap between what the majority of the population want and what a minority imposes upon them. This explains the rising number of protests and the phenomenon of the *Wutbürger* — the citizens certainly have enough reasons to be enraged.

Here are a few examples from many in Europe alone: the unequivocal rejection by French and Dutch voters of the European Constitution in 2005 resulted in just a few minor changes to the law, which was then signed in 2007. Universities' protests against the Bologna Accords was totally disregarded; these accords have now also been imposed, with the predicted negative effects (increase in length of study, lower quality). A third example concerns all activities opposed to the privatisation of healthcare, energy supply, and public transport. A Belgian example: an overwhelming majority of citizens wants an equitable property-tax system, but clearly will not get it. Furthermore, only a small fraction of the Belgian population, around 15 per cent, wants the country to break up along linguistic lines, but the main party in government calls this 'the undercurrent', with the bizarre explanation: 'Flanders is clearly in favour of independence … But I don't know if the Flemish people are ready for independence yet.'[3]

The conclusion is painful: the mechanism that increased the democratic substance of governments for around a century — elections — no longer works. Governments have less and less authority and are operating increasingly openly on the basis of power. If we want to keep it, we must search for a new form of democracy: one that commands a new form of authority.

Forms of democratic government other than those based on elections do indeed exist. Moreover, due to the nature of democracy itself, we must realise that any interpretation of democracy is by definition temporary and will be replaced at some point.

Democracy is always a work in progress

In 1831, a young French nobleman was drawn to America, out of an interest in the new political system there. Some members of his family had ended up at the guillotine during the French Revolution. He himself had entered politics but had not found a home in any of the rival political factions. Alexis de Tocqueville spent a year travelling around America studying the new form of government there. This resulted in 1835 in the publication of his book, known in English as *Democracy in America*, which is still regarded as a standard work today. De Tocqueville's lifelong enthusiasm for this form of government didn't stop him from realising that there is a tension that strains at the heart of democracy. There is an inherent contradiction in the dual ideal of liberty and equality for all men, and thus it can never be realised in full.

A century and a half later, de Tocqueville's countryman Jacques Derrida drew a pragmatic conclusion from that insight. As a political system, democracy strives to provide as much equality as possible to as many people as possible, but, at the same time, it also strives to respect the individual freedom of every single person. In striving for equality, and possibly in imposing it, violence is inflicted on individuals. Conversely, respecting individuality leads to a deterioration of equality. Derrida's pragmatic conclusion was that democracy can never be fully realised; it must always be *la démocratie à venir*, a democracy to come.[4] It comes in stages, with the understanding that there's no definitive endpoint ahead. Democratisation remains a work in progress, but we must always keep the ultimate purpose in mind.*

The purpose is for the *demos*, the people, to govern themselves. This implies that we see all people as politically equal, although we know that they are very different.** Here we see the importance, and even the necessity, of authority. The function of authority (see Hannah Arendt) is to regulate relations between human beings. The authority that goes with democracy aims to regulate those relations in favour of equality while respecting individual freedom.

General elections were an important and extremely valuable stage in the process of democratisation. But that stage is now over. At this time, the effect of elections is even antidemocratic, for several reasons already mentioned. However, there's an even more fundamental reason: on the

---

* The fact that democracy is a continuous process with no definitive endpoint means that the different stages of the democratisation process are always bound to a place and a time (Rosanvallon, 2012). Such an idea has important implications and is, for example, at odds with the idea that 'our' democracy, based on free elections, is the only true democracy and must therefore be imposed on countries that have 'not got there yet'. The results of elections imposed by the West on Afghanistan, Iraq, and various African countries can't be called successful. The historical circumstances are different, and so democracy must take a different form in these places. Moreover, imposing 'our' democracy on others is highly undemocratic and, most significantly, paternalistic.

** Striving for equality has a dangerous side to it, however, since it can be used to justify the imposition of uniformity (if necessary, literally, with actual uniforms) in society. Today, we can best interpret the word *demos* to mean 'the community'.

basis of dictates from non-democratic bodies, governments impose measures on the population that increase inequality. This runs directly counter to the democratic ideal.

For those who might be thinking that this observation is rooted in the political left: the latest report from the OECD finds that inequality is indeed increasing, with negative effects for the economy and for society.[5] At the time of going to press, an International Monetary Fund report has confirmed that increasing income inequality is also very harmful for the economy. If the richest 20 per cent of a country's citizens get 1 per cent richer, the result is a fall in the country's gross domestic product. Conversely, if the 20 per cent with the lowest incomes get 1 per cent less poor, GDP goes up. In an article on this report in the *De Standaard* newspaper, we read: 'The IMF has called on countries to make more frequent use of taxes on property and wealth and to do more to discourage tax evasion.'[6] According to the IMF, if politicians want to promote their country's economy, it's very clear where the savings must be made.[7]

Like many others, I'm convinced that we are currently at a turning point. It took revolutions to get rid of the hereditary aristocracy. Universal suffrage didn't arrive until after many people had died in demonstrations and strikes. During every transitional period, power relations were rearranged, and such development can be towards more democracy (more equality among people) or towards less democracy (more inequality). Inequality is currently increasing and democracy is decreasing, with an increase in resistance and protest. *Wutbürger*.

I described how at the basis of a new authority there is always an original form of violence against the previous authority. We can see that in the growing resistance within society to governments that impose new social relations on it from a position of power. In the best case, we will evolve towards a different interpretation of authority, including in the political sphere. This will require 'legal violence', to use Walter Benjamin's phrase.[8] Let us hope that the violence does not go beyond that.

Power in place of authority

David Van Reybrouck describes our current politic situation as an epidemic of what he calls DFS, democratic fatigue syndrome. Citizens no longer believe in democracy and are ripe for two 'remedies', both of which are worse than the disease itself.

One of these is populism, which poses as democratic, but is not: often, it's necessary for people to die before this becomes clear. Nationalism, a typical type of populism, is raising its head all over Europe. In the classic sense of *Blut und Boden* ('blood and soil'), it has become outdated. But anyone who takes the trouble to examine modern-day nationalism will soon see that it is, in fact, regionalism, and its motives are financial. Economically successful regions (Northern Italy, Catalonia, Flanders) want to break away from less successful regions. What this boils down to is a short-sighted rejection of solidarity.* Many voters don't seem to realise that, sooner or later, they will suffer the same fate as those in less successful regions — mostly much sooner than expected. It's striking how often that, as soon as they get into power, regionalist parties make socioeconomic decisions to the disadvantage of most of their constituents. Often, the new rulers will conceal this by focusing even more on the supposed enemy. Someone else is always to blame.

Seemingly diametrically opposed to the populist remedy, another solution also aims to jettison democracy, by placing power in the hands of a small group of experts — a technocracy, in other words. The reasoning behind this is the precise opposite of populism, which expects 'common sense' to solve everything. The technocratic dream is based on the belief that governing has become so complex that even politicians are no longer able to see the entire picture, let alone take the right decisions. So, those decisions can better be 'outsourced' to experts, whose objective knowledge means they're able to make sound decisions. This reasoning is consistent with modern buzzwords like 'efficiency' and

---

* Dutch sociologist Willem Schinkel (2012) rightly points out that nationalism doesn't by definition have to take on a neoliberal economic form — indeed, the contrary may be true. Scottish nationalists are expressly left-wing. Nationalism can certainly be founded on solidarity between a larger group of people who share a certain history. In what Schinkel calls 'critical nationalism', such solidarity can fit in with a commitment to the wider world, rather than withdrawing into a gated community (which, by its very gated nature, is an invitation to plunderers).

'problem management'. Forget ideology, focus on solutions, and everyone will be happy.

That sounds appealing. Decisions made on the basis of studied analysis and knowledge, with no party-political squabbling; who could have anything against that? Let me give you two examples: fracking for shale gas in the Netherlands, and traffic chaos around Antwerp. Both issues have been on the political agenda for years, and the proposed solutions have gradually become illustrations of this problem: appearing falsely to dig deep, and getting stuck in gridlock. The different solutions proposed are always different results of different 'objective' studies by different experts …

This brings us back to what I described in chapter four. In politics and society, there are no objective studies, and objective figures do not exist. The research methods used may be objective; the research questions and the criteria applied never are. Social questions are always formulated on the basis of an ideological view of the ideal society. The rabbit can't come out of the hat unless we put it there in the first place. Do we give priority to restricting the amount of particulate matter in the air and reducing traffic noise, as well as to making the city liveable? Or do we give priority to port traffic? Should we include the amount of escaped methane gas in our calculations, together with soil contamination by the chemicals used, and their effect on the groundwater? Or should we give priority to the reduction in energy prices and the associated reduced reliance on energy imports?

Before the experts can get to work, certain social

boundaries must be drawn: we want this, we don't want that; this should be given priority, that should not; and so on. Democracy demands that these choices should be based on social consultation, leading to a position that represents the majority view. But such consultations are rare, and people are no longer prepared to accept that. Citizens are taking matters into their own hands and setting their own priorities. Thus, the case of Antwerp's traffic chaos was politically forced open by Ringland, a citizens' group that used crowdfunding to pay to have its own studies carried out, after which they expressly opted for a more liveable city.*

Leaving such decisions to experts is not a good idea. In practice, that means shifting power into the hands of a small group of people who govern beyond any democratic control and make decisions in the interests of the dominant power — currently, the so-called free market. One of the most outrageous examples, which I touched on before, is that of Luxembourg's so-called advance-tax rulings, which are used as a tool for companies to develop strategies for legal tax avoidance. The Dutch professor J.L.M. Gribnau shows in a well-documented presentation how legislators undermine their own authority with such rulings.[9]

---

* See http://ringland.be/grassroots-design-a-large-infrastructure-project/. This is undoubtedly a test case for modern democracy and for the actual application of what politicians are always propagating themselves: public participation of citizens. If politicians continue to push through their own policies regardless, the number of *Wutbürger* in the greater Antwerp area will increase significantly.

The technocratic decision-making process has become much more of a reality than you or I realise. The secret societies of the past have become the not-so-secret societies of today, to paraphrase Ludo Couvreur. Some are more well-known than others, but they all avoid democratic control: the G20, the European Central Bank, the International Monetary Fund, and, most significantly, the big banks. Every year in Davos, heads of government queue up to be told behind closed doors what is expected of them and what they can expect in exchange. There's an important difference between now and the past because the old *omertà* (code of secrecy within criminal organisations) is disappearing, and the number of 'leaks' is increasing — note the negative connotations of that term, by the way.

The transparency that should be normal in democracy is missing, so we citizens have to make do with 'leaks'. LuxLeaks made that patently obvious. When, in November 2014, it was 'leaked' that Luxembourg had entered into favourable tax agreements with numerous multinational companies, various government leaders hastened to point out that there was nothing illegal about those tax rulings. This was true; under pressure from those multinationals and others, legislation had been adjusted so that companies paid almost no tax, with the savings mostly paid for by ordinary taxpayers. The Belgian finance minister demanded, correctly, that the Luxembourg tax rulings be made public. Transparency above all else. In the wake of that scandal, however, it emerged that Belgium had also entered into similar fiscal agreements with 60 multinational companies. The very same minister went before the Belgian parliament to say that the content of the relevant tax rulings would not be released.[10]

The conclusion is clear. The most important decisions in Europe are principally economic, rather than political, in nature. Furthermore, these are decisions that both reduce autonomy and increase inequality, and thus run counter to the aims of democracy (promoting equality and freedom). Many of these decisions are barely, or sometimes not at all, left in the hands of the elected European Parliament, but are actually made by bodies that avoid democratic control. And I haven't even mentioned the impact of expensive lobby groups on political decision-making.*

To repeat: such decisions can never be neutral in nature, despite all the objective-looking spreadsheets. The research those spreadsheets are based on is explicitly ideologically coloured. The social impact of the dominant free-market

---

* A recent example: Most scientists now generally agree about the serious effects of endocrine-disrupting chemicals (EDCs) on human health. The EU wants to restrict their use and tasked a scientific committee with drawing up a list of these dangerous substances. Their study was completed at the end of 2012; in June 2013, the proposal was rejected and the project postponed. The reason for this change of heart has only now become known: lobbying by the chemical industry, led by Bayer. We know this because the Corporate Europe Observatory published a report on the case. This group studies the impact of lobbying on the EU's decision-making process. In this case, messages from Bayer and the times at which they were sent left nothing to the imagination (Horel, 2015). The work of this research group is yet another example of the new social control. For now, it hasn't had much effect, except to once again increase the number of *Wutbürger*.

ideology can be summed up in one word: anti-solidarity. In a democracy, policy options must be presented to the population, preferably with a clear explanation of their consequences. That is becoming less and less the case.

Both the solutions to the political crisis as described — populism and technocracy — lead to the pyramidal exercising of pure power. Along with sociologists like Luc Huyse and Pierre Rosanvallon, I call on citizens to reconquer politics with the aim of de-marketising the society we live in. This will require both a radical change and a new kind of authority. My proposed solution won't come as a surprise: the collective, as a new form of democracy, must build that authority. The key question is what shape that new authority, as the next step in the democratisation process, must take.

Radical change

Before every election, all political parties promise change: after every election, all governments do the same as the one before, just more decisively. There are three changes that need to be made, but are not: (1) a change of power, so that (2) decisions can be remade in the interests of the community, (3) on the basis of a contemporary form of democracy.

First and foremost, a change of power is needed. There's an ever-growing consensus on this: the essential power to make decisions must return to politics and no longer rest with 'the markets'. Recent scandals have made it more than clear that politicians have been eclipsed by the 'free' market.

In the case of LuxLeaks, the exposed rulings were legal, no matter how unethical they were. In the SwissLeaks scandal, this was no longer the case. A software engineer at HSBC (a British bank) handed over digital data concerning secret bank accounts at HSBC's Swiss subsidiary. A consortium of 130 investigative journalists set to work on the data, subsequently uncovering that those accounts held more than €100 billion in connection with tax evasion and fraud. The journalists note that the information released is merely a snapshot and that it's highly likely that the real sums are much bigger. The fraudulent activities branch out all over the world, making it nigh on impossible for national governments to get a grip on them.

The collaboration between the investigative consortium and the software engineer is an illustration of modern-day social control, of which we will see many more examples in the future. The SwissLeaks case once again demonstrates the need for transparency, and, above all, for the ability to impose sanctions (authority without legitimate power does not work).[11] The world economy is in the hands of a very small collection of dominant financial organisations. The result is an erosion of political autonomy, increased inequality, and the destruction of our environment. This list of consequences may sound plaintive, but the evidence is overwhelming.

The second necessary change is that political decisions must once again be made in the interests of the community, and not in the interests of a financial minority. The dismantling of the welfare state under the guise of a false promise of a 'participatory society', combined with a policy of blaming individuals under the pretext of 'everyone must take responsibility for their own lives', means first and foremost that more and more tax money flows into the hands of the tiny minority. Political decisions must now more than ever give priority to environmental issues, once again in the interests of the community. If this doesn't change, there will soon be no future for us to worry about.

For the third essential change, I must assume that your and my preference is still for a democratic form of government. If so, then we must enter a new phase in the democratisation process. How can we give concrete form to this new collective within a political system worthy of the name? The incentives for concrete alternatives sometimes come from unexpected quarters.

The US state of Texas, land of the Lone Star Cowboy, huge steaks, gun-toting conservative rednecks, and nodding donkeys (oil pumps) — do you recognise the clichés? Well, now we must adjust them a little. At the end of the last century, energy companies wanted to consult Texans on essential questions concerning their energy supply ('your energy' is clearly more than just an empty advertising slogan). They came up against the classic problems with plebiscites: what alternatives do you propose, are all citizens sufficiently informed, will lobbyists highjack the referendum? The energy suppliers turned to James Fishkin, professor of communication at Stanford University, for help.

Fishkin's approach has become a milestone in new politics. With what he calls a 'deliberative opinion poll', he laid the foundation for a contemporary interpretation of democracy. 'Deliberative' in this context means 'by consultation'. Consequently, a deliberative democracy is one that's based on consultation. It sounds very simple, but at the same time it's particularly important. I believe this is the next step in the democratisation process, and, in the best-case scenario, deliberative democracy can even provide the non-violent basis for the radical changes that will come, one way or another.

In a nutshell: Fishkin gathered balanced information on the issue from *all* interest groups, information that was only seen as satisfactory when the different groups agreed on this. The information was then presented by neutral trainers to representative groups from the general population in an unhurried, thorough way over an entire weekend. Participants were able to ask any questions they wanted and were given ample time to discuss the issues among themselves. The entire process was accompanied by trained moderators. Finally, a secret ballot was held, and all participants were aware that the results would be binding. Fishkin organised a total of eight such sessions across the state with the aim of achieving as representative a sample of participants as possible. And the result? Today, Texas is number two among US states for wind power, and the proportion of people who are prepared to pay more for energy from renewable sources has risen from 43 to 84 per cent.

Fishkin's method offers a remedy for the cynicism of our time. Provide people with enough information, let them discuss it among themselves, let them know that their opinion is important and will have a real impact on policy, and you will see remarkable things happen. Thanks to the information they received and the discussions they took part in, many participants had a different, more considered opinion at the end of the process than at the start. The choice they are then able to make — by voting — very often turns out to be in the interests of the general community, and runs directly counter to the individualistic world view of *Homo economicus*. The deliberative democracy model is well on the way to becoming a worldwide success.

Deliberative decision-making about renewable energy is a nice example, but — I assume — not political enough for many readers. An example that's directly connected to politics comes from the United Kingdom. In 2010, a representative group of 130 British people came together over a period of two days to consider, again on the basis of information presented, what political reforms were most needed. Twenty-nine proposals received a clear majority and are expected to form the basis for reforms in the future.[12]

Still not political enough? Then, as a finale, an example of how deliberative polling could have helped change an electoral system. In two Canadian provinces (British Columbia in 2004 and Ontario in 2006), the provincial government let citizens come up with proposals for electoral reform. Both programs ran for almost a year, participants received a fair remuneration, and their proposal was binding in nature. From the outset, politicians decided the proposal would be implemented if it was also approved by a referendum. In both provinces, there was a reasoned proposal, but these didn't receive the necessary two-thirds majority of votes in the subsequent referendums. In 2006, the government in the Netherlands organised a similar, albeit more limited, deliberative poll on electoral reform. One important way it differed from the Canadian examples was that the proposal was not binding and, after it was finished (in 2008), it disappeared into a drawer somewhere.*

The Canadian experiment shows where the weakness lies: in the transition from a deliberative poll to a classic referendum. In a classic referendum, the voter doesn't have the information or the opportunity for consultation provided by the deliberative-poll approach, and so you get a large group of people deciding on an issue they know very little about. And then the probability that a plebiscite will deliver an ill-considered reaction is very high. This is precisely what does not happen with a deliberative process, where a significant number of participants come to a well-considered decision based on information and consultation. To put proposals based on deliberative democracy to the vote in a classic referendum is simply a contradiction in terms.

That brings us to fundamental questions. What is the democratic content of the deliberative approach? What place do elections have in it? Who determines which policy options should be put to a deliberative poll? And

---

* This and other examples are discussed in detail by David Van Reybrouck in his appeal for a new kind of democracy, *Against Elections*. Concerning the Dutch example: I suspect that many Dutch people are not aware that this process even took place, which — I believe — shows that the government at the time didn't want to publicise it. Indeed, it takes courage to organise something that you know will limit your own power.

most importantly: what kind of authority is at work in the deliberative approach?

The democratic content of the deliberative approach

A democratic government almost always operates via a group that deliberates and makes decisions in the name of the entire community. So-called direct democracy, in which everyone is involved in decision-making, only works in small communities (less than 150 people). In larger-scale communities, direct democracy often leads to referendums and plebiscites. They create a semblance of democracy, but in practice they can hardly be called democratic at all. The choice of alternatives on offer and the wording used to present them determine the outcome. Information campaigns are mostly pure propaganda, with little real information. Thus, the crucial question for a democracy centres on the way in which a group of leaders is created. In concrete terms: the democratic content of a government stands or falls by the extent to which the group of leaders is representative of the entire community.

To this day, we try to achieve this by means of elections, presuming that universal suffrage guarantees that the results will be representative of society at large. This presumption is questionable in itself (until recently, for example, half the population, women, were massively underrepresented in government); the way elections are organised today means it's certainly questionable whether they result in a government that is representative of society.

Another method that dates from a bygone age, and which has recently been revived, is choosing citizens by drawing lots. G1000, an initiative launched by the writer David Van Reybrouck, brought together thousands of citizens in this way to come up with a new Belgian constitution. But I prefer deliberative polling.

Deliberative democracy does not make use of elections, but works on the principle of proportional representation, based on simple calculations using transparent criteria. The aim is to put together a group that's as close a reflection of the community as possible. A community's diversity determines the criteria for creating the group: equal numbers of men and women, a range of ages and levels of education that mirrors that of society, as well as other important considerations (for example, geographical distribution and linguistic groups).

A group put together in this way undoubtedly presents a representative picture of society, which means its democratic content is high. Furthermore, the format of a deliberative poll provides a fine answer to a number of problems in politics today. For example: consultations are led by moderators, which means the group can't be hijacked by populist leaders. Party political posturing and infighting are no longer an issue. The distribution to the group of information from a diverse range of sources is both an answer to the one-sided planning of ideologically driven experts, and a defence against lobbying. After information has been distributed, a process of broad consultation begins within the group, which results in a well-considered decision supported collectively by everyone.*

Nowadays, many voters believe their vote doesn't matter. Deliberative democracy restores citizens' faith that they are being heard and that they can influence policy, as it should be in a democracy. The experiences of profit-driven commons/cooperatives of the Semco type teach us that such groups are even prepared to 'make sacrifices' and that the painful measures they propose themselves have much stronger support.

Thus, any criticism that says this approach isn't democratic enough is nonsense. The opposite is true: these days, bodies meant to represent the people that are voted in through elections are far from representative of the population, allow themselves to be led by interests that aren't those of the community, and therefore rightly

---

* A small-scale example: in Antwerp, a construction project was opposed by a neighbourhood committee. Instead of launching the usual legal campaign, the project developer withdrew the planning application and sat down with the committee face to face. Three months later, a plan was ready and had the full support of the neighbourhood. The local residents had discussed the issue among themselves for months, so they were very familiar with the case and knew what their demands were. The following year, in 2013, the same construction developer planned another large-scale project and involved the neighbourhood from the outset. It's notable that local politicians were *not* invited to join the consultation, because — according to the neighbourhood committee — they were mainly interested in scoring political points. This and other examples are described by Luc Huyse (2014) as he offers solutions to today's political crisis. I don't think I'm doing his considerations any disservice by lumping his solutions together under the heading of 'deliberative democracy'.

command less and less trust among voters. If we still want to have elections, they must not be aimed at voting in a supposedly representative group, since there are much better ways of achieving that aim.

In future, citizens should be given the opportunity to vote for certain points of policy (and against others), so that it becomes clear which policies are supported by a majority of the population. Instead of a few hundred names on a ballot paper, voters should be given a choice between 80 policy options, for example. This would mean election campaigns would be about distributing specific information on those policy points. The policies that receive a clear majority of votes would directly determine the agenda of the executive power, which would indeed once again become just that, an executive power.

How the executive power (the government) and the legislative power (the parliament) should then be put together, and what role political parties should play in that, is another matter. David Van Reybrouck discusses various possibilities that combine an elected group, a scientifically assembled representative group, and persons who are appointed by drawing lots. A large body of research shows that alternative models (viz. those not based merely on electing individual people) are both conceivable and achievable. The main difficulty in changing the current political system is resistance from political parties. They will have to not only face fundamental questions about their existence, but also admit, and preferably promote, those changes.

Who sets the agenda?

Anyone with policy-setting experience, from members of sports-club steering committees to holders of a political mandate, knows how important an agenda is. Just as the media determine what is 'news', an agenda determines which policy issues should be addressed. Furthermore, the way an item on an agenda is formulated is crucial (the way we formulate a problem steers the solution in a certain direction). A democratic government must take great care that its policy concerns are the same as those that keep the community awake at night. There is great reason to think that the agendas of Western governments are set by non-democratic organisations, with formulations of problems that are not in line with the desires of the community. Taking back control of the decision-making process means taking back political control of the agenda.

I presume readers will now be asking themselves whether such a common agenda is really feasible. Some time ago, I was asked what I thought of the election platform of a Flemish political party. It so happened that I had just been examining the election platform of a different party very closely. To my amazement, there were far more similarities between the policies of the two parties than differences. Professor Timothy Garton Ash writes that 70–80 per cent of the policies of all UK political parties are the same (he calls it 'the boring truth'), although parties continue to fight tooth and nail. We can draw two conclusions from this. Firstly, that a common agenda *is* feasible. And secondly, that parties aren't the best organisations to implement that agenda. Politicians are out to 'score points' at the cost of their political rivals, and that leads them to lose sight of what is in the general interest.

Of all the authors I consulted, only the sociologist Willem Schinkel dealt explicitly with the issue of agenda-setting, in his book *De nieuwe democratie* (*The New Democracy*). According to him, the political agenda is set by a combination of the media and the market — although for the sake of completeness, I must add that the media have now become subject to the market (they don't sell newspapers to readers, they sell readers to advertisers). Schinkel's solution consists of establishing a fourth power, alongside the executive, legislative, and judicial powers, which would be the agenda-setting power. Creating such a power could give new meaning to the State Council or the Senate, in which — again according to Schinkel — representatives from the worlds of art, religion, and science should also be given a say.

In itself, the creation of such a body is doubtless an excellent and even necessary idea. The inspiration for a new type of agenda-setting could even be much broader and could make use of modern software that offers a good combination of representative and direct democracy: LiquidFeedback. This open-source software was developed in 2010 and provides a clear summary of the issues that a (very) large group of citizens find important. Moreover, the program can also be used for decision-making.[13]

A political agenda must reflect what a community considers important. Schinkel rightly points out the necessity of separating his new, fourth power from the other three, to prevent corruption and a concentration of power. Unfortunately, the classic and democratically necessary separation of powers (in which the Belgian constitution once played an exemplary role) has more or less disappeared. The legislative power (the parliament) mainly does what the executive power (the government) dictates and not the other way round, as was originally intended. Meanwhile, the judicial power is becoming increasingly coloured by party politics due to political appointments. This is also a problem that can be tackled by a rational, representative collection of policy institutions — representative, that is, of the people, not of the political parties.

Moreover, the question of the composition of the agenda-setting power is connected to that of the geographical scope of its decisions. The classic nation-states may adopt laws that, for example, require multinationals to comply with social legislation on their territory, but those states will lose out if that company decides to move its residence to a low-wage country — where social protection is virtually non-existent. The consequences are well known: nation-states compete with one another to offer tax breaks to multinationals, at the expense of their own people. They compete with each other to dismantle the protection of their own voters and allow exploitation once more. This is known as 'the race to the bottom'. The irony reaches its peak when we see that even national trade unions refuse to show solidarity with trade unions from other countries, because they must 'protect their own branches'. The way 19th-century industrialists played off their workers against each other is now being repeated on an international level.

Joining in with such a negative auction is tantamount to signing your own death warrant. There's always someone more desperate than you, and there will always be someone willing to do your job for an even lower wage than you.

This is why the geographical scope of decisions is important. Developments in this area have continued long enough for a clear pattern to have emerged. In politics, the nation-states are evaporating and decisions are being taken by the EU. In society, the countryside is disappearing and cities are becoming the dominant type of community. On the one hand, as cities develop, an important local decision-making space develops along with them; on the other hand, a global decision-making space already exists with Europe.

All around the world, cities are taking the lead in the areas of environmental protection, traffic and transport, healthcare, and governance. There's no doubt that they create their own political dynamics. They discovered the importance of deliberative consultation some time ago, often in combination with grass-roots initiatives. That's not difficult to understand: the distance between citizens and the government is smaller in cities, and local governments — notwithstanding a few exceptions — are much more inclined to listen to their populations than national governments are. The measures taken by a city government can also be very specific and connect the needs of a particular area at a particular time. The one-size-fits-all model of top-down national governments takes no account of local circumstances and mainly provokes resistance. Cities must be allowed to set their own agenda and act on it, based on their own policy-making organisations.

However, if the decision-making space remains limited to that local environment, we will soon return to medieval-type wars between city-states. There is still a need for overarching regulations to determine a limited number of outlines, which cities can then interpret as they see fit. These outlines must be both sufficiently broad and mandatory, and they must be principally social in character. In line with the concept of horizontal authority, cities are now busy setting up so-called global covenants, in which they sign up to a climate-neutral policy, for example. The EU of countries may soon face stiff competition from the EU of cities.

The collective as political authority

Politics, too, needs a new basis for authority. That this should be the collective is blatantly obvious: in a democratic system, it goes without saying that government is carried out by a representative group. I believe that this group's authority will become horizontal in nature, with representative groups of citizens both setting the agenda and taking decisions on the basis of consultation. The new politicians will have a new function: facilitating this process, ensuring that citizens receive correct and balanced information, protecting the majority from the impact of a powerful minority, and making sure the decisions taken are implemented.

Traditional politicians speak to 'the electorate' or, even worse, to the 'citizens as customers', and fail to recognise sufficiently that new groups of people who choose a different kind of society are springing up everywhere. Real local communities such as cities and regions are being joined by digital communities with a potentially transnational character. Today's governments speak to individuals, while everywhere a new 'we' is growing, which is able to organise itself both digitally and in the real world.

I think the chances are high that change will emerge from actual practice, rather than, as in the past, a top-down ideology and its associated great narrative. The actual practice will be concerned with concrete areas such as the environment, energy, drinking-water supply, housing, traffic and transport, education, healthcare, and employment. The motivation for change is more than obvious: to judge by psychosocial health indicators, more and more people are doing less and less well (in *all* social strata, even the top levels).[14] This is not so strange, considering the consequences of modern work practices: mistrust, helplessness, insecurity, cut-throat competition, long-term unemployment, chronic lack of time, burnout, loneliness, and existential angst. And this, at a time when people more than ever have a need for trust, solidarity, self-determination, cooperation, and meaning in their lives. A society that can provide those things will have far lower rates of illness and joblessness, and an economy that's better in every respect. To make this a reality, we need a new kind of politics, which brings about *real* change.

CONCLUSION

I am who I am through my relationships with others —
my parents and my children, my superiors at work and
my colleagues, the opposite sex. I became myself in and
through all those exchanges of love and of hate. Authority
has as its function the regulation of those relations, a
regulating force to which everyone submits (some more
willingly than others) to make the world a liveable, and
preferably also a pleasant, environment. The importance of
that function is huge.

The question of whether we are good or bad can be
answered clearly by looking at history. We are capable
of both good and evil. The society in which we build
our identity determines how we relate to others. Since
we are the only species that substantially influences its
surroundings, we are able to steer ourselves in any direction
whatsoever. Nevertheless, we should not forget that we are
primarily social animals, focused on each other. Studies
of young children reveal surprising results: prosocial
behaviour (helping others) comes about spontaneously;
antisocial behaviour must be learned. Young children

will spontaneously come to the aid of someone in need. If they're rewarded for doing so, after a time they will only help others if there's a reward associated with that behaviour.[1]

These and other findings show that we must pay attention to the way in which our society and the authority associated with it are organised. Classic pyramidal authority based on the fear of hell and damnation combined with ignorance is in need of replacement. My preference is for horizontal authority based on knowledge — shared, transparent knowledge, combined with a new kind of fear — fear of social control.

Upbringing and education, gender and sexuality, economics and politics — all imply authority, because every one of them concerns relations between people. The kind of authority I put forward in this book is neither a technology (although it can make use of certain technologies) nor an institution (although it means we'll have to rethink some of our institutions). It's a conviction based on changes that are already happening today. In the best-case scenario, authority based in horizontally organised groups will become part of our identity, just as authority based on a patriarchal pyramid once was.

The autonomy of the individual will be central to this authority, given its horizontal nature, but that autonomy must necessarily be combined with solidarity with others. Autonomy in solidarity doesn't rest on a belief in the 'noble savage' who only needs the community occasionally before going back to his beloved nature. Autonomy in solidarity certainly doesn't mean the supposed spontaneous self-regulation of a group — that would be nothing more than a variation on the belief in the invisible hand. For a collective to be able to function as the basis for authority, a number of conditions must be explicitly met. These have been described in different ways by Haim Omer, Ricardo Semler, and Elinor Ostrom, and can also be found in many proposals for political reform.

These conditions are not utopian flights of fancy; they are certainly not a blueprint for a future paradise to be imposed on people by force. Anyone who cares to look around will see that change is already underway. This strengthens my belief that a horizontal authority is indeed becoming the new form of authority. The question is not whether these changes will take place, but how we can support this process that is already happening, and which powers will try to stop them.

ACKNOWLEDGEMENTS

What I have written is not original. All of it has already been written elsewhere by other people. Just like an identity, a book is always made up of bits of other books, with what was left out being as important as what was included. This is mainly through an unconscious process, but, fortunately for me, in this case it also involved some real exchanges.

Both I and this book owe a great deal to Philipp Blom and Erwin Mortier. Their knowledge and their criticism, always wrapped up in humour, raised *Says Who?* to a higher level. And the culinary skills of both undoubtedly also played a part in that.

I made the acquaintance of Ludo Couvreur in the wake of my last book's publication. His knowledge of economics and philosophy were a genuine help to me, as was his assistance with much research work.

Dominiek Hoens led me back to an old love of mine, Blaise Pascal. Silvia Janssens pointed out a significant omission on my part: I had not planned a chapter on gender — in a book about the decline of the patriarchy!

Joachim Cauwe helped research the impact of that decline on homosexuality and gender relations. Fientje Moerman supplied me with correct information about the legislative changes concerning baby naming (and in between times also recommended the work of Yuval Harari to me). Johan Mertens remains a dialogue partner for social biology. Katleen De Stobbeleir provided me with information about horizontal leadership. Christien Brinkgreve was ahead of me once again with her study of the return of authority. Wouter Van Driessche practically forced me to read Baricco's *The Barbarians*.

Piet and Johan, my running companions and partners in crime, were my best readers — it's definitely not a good idea to reproduce their comments here, but let's just say that I enjoyed them very much. The comments from my sister Christine and from Eline Trenson inspired me to rewrite some passages to make them clearer.

Dialogue with some others took place via their publications. I gained a lot from reading the works of Luc Huyse, Thomas Decreus, Marc Reynebeau, Willem Schinkel, and David Van Reybrouck. Hannah Arendt is a permanent source of inspiration.

My main dialogue partner is also my life partner, Rita, who has had to listen to more about authority over the past few years than she would probably have liked, I fear …

This is a book that looks to the past but is really about the future, and that is why I dedicate it to Luce, my granddaughter.

BIBLIOGRAPHY

Abicht, L. *Democratieën sterven liggend. Kritiek van de tactische rede.* Antwerp: Houtekiet, 2014.

Appignanesi, L. *Mad, Bad, and Sad: a history of women and the mind doctors from 1800 to the present.* London: Virago, 2008.

Arendt, H. 'What Is Authority?'. 1954. http://la.utexas.edu/ users/hcleaver/330T/350kPEEArendtWhatIsAuthorityTa ble.pdf

Bajaj, V. 'Micro Lenders, honoured with Nobel, are struggling', *The New York Times*, 6 January 2011.

Baricco, A. *The Barbarians.* New York: Rizzoli Ex Libris, 2013.

Bauman, Z. & Lyon, D. *Liquid Surveillance: a conversation.* Cambridge: Polity Press, 2013.

Bauwens, M. & Lievens, J. *De wereld redden. Met peer-to-peer naar een postkapitalistische samenleving.* Antwerp/Utrecht: Houtekiet, 2013.

Benjamin, W. 'Capitalism as Religion' (fragment, translated by C. Kautzer) in: Mendieta E. (ed.) *The Frankfurt School on Religion.* New York: Routledge, 2005.

———. 'Critique of Violence' (translated by E. Jephcott) in: Demetz, P. (ed.) *Reflections.* New York: Schocken, 1976.

Blom, P. *Wicked Company: freethinkers and friendship in pre-revolution Paris.* London: Weidenfeld Nicholson, 2011.

Boehm, C. 'Egalitarian Behaviour and Reverse Dominance Hierarchy', *Current Anthropology*, 1993, 34(3), pp. 227–254.

Bogle, K. *Hooking Up: sex, dating, and relationships on campus.* New York: New York University Press, 2008.

Bregman, R. *Geschiedenis van de vooruitgang.* Amsterdam: De Bezige Bij, 2013.

——. *Gratis geld voor iedereen.* Amsterdam: De Correspondent, 2014.

Brinkgreve, C. 'Gezag en Veilige Publieke Taak' in: *Gezag en veiligheid in het openbaar bestuur.* The Hague: Ministry of the Interior and Kingdom Relations (Netherlands), 2014, pp. 21–35.

——. *Het verlangen naar gezag. Over vrijheid, gelijkheid en verlies van houvast.* Amsterdam/Antwerp: Atlas Contact, 2012.

British Psychological Society. 'Response to the American Psychiatric Association: DSM-5 Development'. June 2011. http://apps.bps.org.uk/_publicationfiles/consultation-responses/dsm-5%202011%20-%20BPS%20response.pdf

Catalyst. *The Bottom Line: connecting corporate performance and gender diversity.* 2004. http://www.catalyst.org/knowledge/bottom-line-connecting-corporate-performance-and-gender-diversity

Chavannes, M. *Niemand regeert. Op naar de privatisering van de Nederlandse politiek.* Amsterdam: Nieuw Amsterdam, 2009.

Chua, A. *Battle Hymn of a Tiger Mother.* London: Penguin, 2011.

Claeys, M. *Stilstand. Over machtspolitiek, betweterbestuur en achterkamerdemocratie.* Leuven: Halewyck, 2013.

Crul, M.R.J. et al. *Superdiversiteit. Een nieuwe visie op integratie.* Amsterdam: CASA/VU University Press, 2013.

Dabla-Norris, E. et al. 'Causes and Consequences of Income Inequality: A Global Perspective', International Monetary Fund, 15 June 2015. http://www.imf.org/external/pubs/cat/longres.aspx?sk=42986.0

de Vos, J. *Psychologisation in Times of Globalisation.* London: Routledge, 2012.

de Waal, F. *Good Natured: the origins of right and wrong in humans and other animals.* Cambridge: Harvard University Press, 1996.

——. *The Bonobo and the Atheist: in search of humanism among the primates.* New York: WW Norton, 2013.

de Walsche, A. 'Elinor Ostrom: Een Nobelprijs voor groepswerk', *Oikos*, 2010, 53, pp. 6–12.

Decreus, T. *Een paradijs waait uit de storm. Over macht, democratie en verzet.* Antwerp: EPO, 2013.

Dehue, T. *Betere mensen. Over gezondheid als keuze en koopwaar.* Amsterdam/Antwerp: Uitgeverij Augustus, 2014.

Derrida, J. 'Force of Law: the "mystical foundation of authority"' (translated by M. Quaintance) in: Cornell, D. et al. (eds) *Deconstruction and the Possibility of Justice.* New York: Routledge, 1992.

Desmet, M. 'Experimental Versus Naturalistic Psychotherapy Research: consequences for researchers, clinicians, policy makers, and patients', *Psychoanalytische Perspectieven*, 2013, 31(1), pp. 59–78.

Diamond, J. *Collapse: how societies choose to fail or succeed.* London: Allen Lane, 2005.

Dinardo, R.L. *Germany's Panzer Arm in World War II.*
Mechanicsburg, Pennsylvania: Stackpole Books, 2006.

Du Caju, P. et al. 'De schuldenlast van de huishoudens: verloop
en verdeling', *Economisch Tijdschrift*, September 2014, pp.
65–85.

Elias, N. *The Civilising Process.* Oxford: Blackwell, 1969.

Finkielkraut, A. *L'identité malherueuse.* Paris: Éditions Stock,
2013.

Fishkin, J.S. 'The Nation in a Room: turning public opinion
into policy', *Boston Review*, 1 March 2006. http://
bostonreview.net/james-fishkin-nation-in-a-room-turning-
public-opinion-into-policy

Freud, S. 'A Child Is Being Beaten' in: *The Standard Edition of
the Complete Psychological Works of Sigmund Freud.* London:
Hogarth Press, 1953, vol. 17.

——. 'Family Romances' in: *The Standard Edition of the
Complete Psychological Works of Sigmund Freud.* London:
Hogarth Press, 1953, vol. 9.

——. 'Preface to Aichhorn's *Wayward Youth*' in: *The Standard
Edition of the Complete Psychological Works of Sigmund Freud.*
London: Hogarth Press, 1953, vol. 19.

——. *Civilisation and Its Discontents* in: *The Standard Edition of
the Complete Psychological Works of Sigmund Freud.* London:
Hogarth Press, 1953, vol. 21.

——. *Group Psychology and the Analysis of the Ego* in: *The
Standard Edition of the Complete Psychological Works of
Sigmund Freud.* London: Hogarth Press, 1953, vol. 18.

——. *Moses and Monotheism* in: *The Standard Edition of the
Complete Psychological Works of Sigmund Freud.* London:
Hogarth Press, 1953, vol. 23.

———. *Totem and Taboo* in: *The Standard Edition of the Complete Psychological Works of Sigmund Freud*. London: Hogarth Press, 1953, vol. 13.

Furedi, F. *Authority: a sociological history*. Cambridge: Cambridge University Press, 2013.

———. *Wasted: why education isn't educating*. London: Continuum, 2009.

Garton Ash, T. 'If Britain wants change that counts, there's an election it can vote in today', *The Guardian*, 20 January 2010. https://www.theguardian.com/commentisfree/2010/jan/20/britain-change-counts-election-today

Gerzema, J. & D'Antonio, M. *The Athena Doctrine: how women (and the men who think like them) will rule the future*. San Francisco: John Wiley & Sons, 2013.

Gotlieb, A. et al. *Operatie 'werk Arthur de deur uit'. Dagboek van een ongewenste werknemer*. Amsterdam: Bertram + de Leeuw Uitgevers, 2014.

Gribnau, J. *Belastingen en Ethiek: De ethische dimensie van tax planning*. Reading on 21 February 2013 to mark the opening of the Antwerp Tax Academy.

Hamilton, L. & Armstrong, E.A. 'Gendered Sexuality in Young Adulthood: double binds and flawed options', *Gender and Society*, 2009, 23(5), pp. 589–616. http://faculty2.ucmerced.edu/lhamilton2/docs/paper-2009-gendered-sexuality.pdf

Harari, Y.N. *Sapiens: a brief history of humankind*. London: Vintage Books, 2011.

Hayek, F. 'The Pretence of Knowledge: lecture to the memory of Alfred Nobel'. Stockholm, 11 December 1974. http://www.nobelprize.org/nobel_prizes/economic-sciences/laureates/1974/hayek-lecture.html

Hekma, G. *Homoseksualiteit in Nederland van 1730 tot de moderne tijd*. Amsterdam: Meulenhoff, 2004.

Hermanns, J. *Het opvoeden verleerd*. Amsterdam: UvA/ Vossiuspers, 2009.

Horel, S. *A Toxic Affair: how the chemical lobby blocked action on hormone disrupting chemicals*, May 2015. http:// corporateeurope.org/sites/default/files/toxic_lobby_edc.pdf

Hunter, J. 'The Interest Rate Myth in Indian Microfinance', *Forbes India Magazine*, 9 February 2011, 2011.

Huyse, L. *De democratie voorbij*. Leuven: Van Halewyck, 2014.

Ieven, B. 'Geweld en legitimiteit: over de fundering van het recht bij Rawls en Derrida', *Ethiek & Maatschappij*, 2005, 8(1), pp. 45–57.

Illouz, E. *Why Loves Hurts: a sociological explanation*. Cambridge: Polity Press, 2012.

International Labour Organisation. *World Employment and Social Outlook. Trends 2015*. Geneva. http://www.ilo.org/global/ research/global-reports/weso/2015/lang--en/index.htm

Kant, I. 'Auswahl aus den Reflexionen, Vorarbeiten und Briefen Kants' in: Batscha, Z. (ed.), *Materialien zu Kants Rechtsphilosophie*. Frankfurt: Suhrkamp, 1968

——. 'What is the Enlightenment?' 1784.

Kojève, A. *The Notion of Authority*. London: Verso Books, 2014.

Konner, M. *The Tangled Wing: biological constraints on the human spirit*. Harmondsworth: Penguin, 1984.

Lacan, J. *Les complexes familiaux dans la formation de l'individu*. Paris: Navarin, 1984.

——. *The Seminar of Jacques Lacan, Book VII: The Ethics of Psychoanalysis, 1959–1960* (translated by D. Porter). London: Routledge, 1992.

Laeven, L. & Valencia, F. 'Systemic Banking Crisis Database', *IMF Economic Review*, 2013, 61, pp. 225–270.

Laland, K.N. & Brown, G.R. *Sense and Nonsense: evolutionary perspectives on human behaviour.* Oxford: Oxford University Press.

Le Bon, G. *Psychologie des foules.* 1895. http://www.infoamerica. org/documentos_pdf/lebon2.pdf

Lightdale, J.R. & Prentice, D.A. 'Rethinking Sex Differences in Aggression: aggressive behaviour in the absence of social roles', *Personality and Social Psychology Bulletin*, 1994, 20(1), pp. 34–44.

LSE. *The Depression Report: a new deal for depression and anxiety disorders.* 2006. http://eprints.lse.ac.uk/818/1/ DEPRESSION_REPORT_LAYARD.pdf

——. *Mental Health Promotion and Prevention: the economic case.* 2011. http://www.lse.ac.uk/businessAndConsultancy/ lseenterprise/pdf/pssrufeb2011.pdf

MacIntyre, A. *After Virtue: a study in moral theory.* London: Duckworth, 2007.

Marinova, J. et al. *Gender Diversity and Firm Performance: evidence from Dutch and Danish boardrooms.* Utrecht: Utrecht School of Economics, Utrecht University, 2010.

Maus, M. 'Het nadeel van de twijfel', *De Tijd*, 12 December 2014.

Mazzucato, M. *The Entrepreneurial State: debunking public vs private sector myths.* London: Anthem Press, 2013.

Mertens, P. *Hoe durven ze?* Antwerp: EPO, 2011.

Micklethwait, J. & Wooldridge, A. *The Fourth Revolution: the global race to reinvent the state.* London: Allen Lane, 2014.

Moloney, P. *The Therapy Industry: the irresistible rise of the talking cure and why it doesn't work*. London: Pluto Press, 2013.

Morrens, M. 'Routine outcome monitoring in Vlaanderen: leren we wel de juiste lessen uit het Nederlandse gerommel?', *Tijdschrift voor psychiatrie*, 2015, 57, pp. 392–394. http://www.tijdschriftvoorpsychiatrie.nl/assets/articles/57-2015-6-artikel-morrens.pdf

OECD. *Education at a Glance 2011: OECD indicators*. http://www.oecd.org/education/school/educationataglance2011oecdindicators.htm

———. *In It Together: why less inequality benefits all*. 2015. http://www.oecd.org/social/in-it-together-why-less-inequality-benefits-all-9789264235120-en.htm

———. *The Future of Families to 2030: a synthesis report*. 2011. http://www.oecd.org/futures/49093502.pdf

Omer, H. *The New Authority: family, school, and community*. Cambridge: Cambridge University Press, 2010.

Orwell, G. 'Notes on Nationalism'. 1945. http://orwell.ru/library/essays/nationalism/english/e_nat

Pascal, B. *Pensées* (translated by W.F. Trotter). New York: EP Dutton, 1958.

Peeters, J. 'De *commons*. Een beperkte gids naar recente literatuur', *Oikos*, 2014, 70, pp. 41–49.

Pels, D. *Het volk bestaat niet. Leiderschap en populisme in de mediademocratie*. Amsterdam: De Bezige Bij, 2011.

Pinxten, R. *Schoon protest. Want er is wel een alternatief*. Antwerp: EPO, 2014.

Polgreen, L. & Bajaj, V. 'India Microcredit faces collapse from defaults', *The New York Times*, 17 November 2010.

Ramzi, A. 'De vraag om gezag', opinion article in

de Volkskrant, 8 May 2010. http://www.happychaos.nl/
gezag-in-de-volkskrant/

Rawls, J. *A Theory of Justice*. Cambridge: Belknap, 1971.

Rifkin, J. *The Zero Marginal Cost Society: the internet of things,
the collaborative commons, and the eclipse of capitalism*. New
York: Palgrave-MacMillan, 2014.

Rosanvallon, P. *Democratie en tegendemocratie*. Amsterdam:
Boom/Stichting Internationale Spinozalens, 2012.

Rosin, H. *The End of Men and the Rise of Women*. London:
Viking, 2013.

Ross, C. *The Leaderless Revolution: how ordinary people will take
power and change politics in the 21st century*. London: Simon
and Schuster, 2011.

Rotmans, J. & de Zutter, J. 'Het zijn de burgers die aan het stuur
zitten', *Samenleving en politiek*, March 2013, pp. 20–30. http://
www.stichtinggerritkreveld.be/samenleving-en-politiek/
zoeken-in-sampol/128-2013/maart-1017/1017het-zijn-de-
burgers-die-aan-het-stuur-zitten

Roubini, N. & Mihm, S. *Crisis Economics: a crash course in the
future of finance*. London: Allen Lane, 2010.

Schaubroeck, K. *Een verpletterend gevoel van
verantwoordelijkheid*. Breda, Netherlands: De Geus, 2010.

Schinkel, W. *De nieuwe democratie. Naar andere vormen van
politiek*. Amsterdam: De Bezige Bij, 2012.

Semler, R. *Maverick!: the success story behind the world's most
unusual workplace*. London: Arrow, 1993.

Sennett, R. *Authority*. London: Secker & Warburg, 1980.

——. *The Fall of Public Man*. London: Penguin, 2002.

Serres, M. *Thumbelina: the culture and technology of millennials*.
London: Rowman and Littlefield, 2014.

Torfs, W. *Werken met hart en ziel. Bouwstenen voor een great place to work*. Tielt, Belgium: LannooCampus, 2014.

van Bezien, I. et al. 'Going, Going … Gone?: the decline of party membership in contemporary Europe', *European Journal of Political Research*, 2012, 51(1), pp. 24–56.

van der Lans, J. *Koning Burger. Nederland als zelfbedieningszaak*. Amsterdam: Uitgeverij Augustus, 2011.

Van Driessche, W. *Modern Minds. Kan uw hoofd de 21ste eeuw aan?* Brussels: Mediafin, 2014.

Van Hoorde, H. 'Statistiatrie, nosologie en structuur: één vraag?', *Tijdschrift voor Psychiatrie*, 1986, 1, pp. 6–14.

Van Reybrouck, D. *Against Elections*. London: Bodley Head, 2016.

van Stigt, M. *Alles over pesten*. Amsterdam: Boom, 2014.

Vanheule, S. *Diagnosis and the DSM: a critical review*. London: Palgrave Macmillan, 2014.

Verbeet, G. *Vertrouwen is goed maar begrijpen is beter. Over de vitaliteit van onze parlementaire democratie*. Amsterdam: Singel Uitgeverijen, 2012.

Verhaeghe, P. 'Chronicle of a Death Foretold: the end of psychotherapy'. 2007. http://www.paulverhaeghe.com/lecturesandinterviews/DublinHealth4life.pdf

——. *Mijn idee voor Nederland*. 2013. http://paulverhaeghe.psychoanalysis.be/lezingen/Amsterdamdebaliedec2013.pdf

Versnel, H. & Brouwer, J.J. *Stop de Amerikanen! Ten minste tien goede redenen om gewoon Europees te blijven*. Houten: Terra Lannoo, 2011.

Warneken, F. & Tomasello, M. 'The Roots of Human Altruism', *British Journal of Psychology*, 2009, 100, pp. 455–471.

Weber, M. *The Protestant Ethic and the Spirit of Capitalism.* New York: Norton, 2009.

Welzer, H. *Selbst denken. Eine Anleitung zum Widerstand.* Frankfurt: Fischer, 2013.

WHO. *Mental Health, Resilience, and Inequalities.* Copenhagen, 2009. http://www.euro.who.int/__data/assets/pdf_file/0012/100821/E92227.pdf

Wilkinson, R. & Pickett, K. *The Spirit Level: why equality is better for everyone.* London: Penguin, 2010.

Young, M. *The Rise of the Meritocracy 1870–2033: an essay on education and equality.* London: Penguin, 1958.

Young-Bruehl, E. *Hannah Arendt: for love of the world.* New Haven: Yale University Press, 1982.

Zonderop, Y. *Polderen 3.0. Nederland en het algemeen belang.* Leusden, Netherlands: De Vrije Uitgevers, 2012.

NOTES

Chapter One: Identity and Authority

1   If we were to transfer our entire monthly salary to the state until
    all our taxes for the year were paid, 'tax freedom day' would be the
    day on which we reached that point and after which our entire
    salary would belong to us each month. The idea is abused (mostly
    by free-market politicians) to criticise the government (they call
    taxes 'government seizure') for allegedly bleeding hardworking
    citizens dry. The most common comparison is with the US, where
    citizens pay much less tax and 'tax freedom day' comes months
    earlier in the calendar than many other countries. What those
    politicians forget to mention is what citizens get in return for
    their taxes. And what citizens in the US don't get. I invite anyone
    to research the cost of a university education in the US, or a
    course of medical treatment, and to check the condition of public
    infrastructure such as roads or the electricity distribution network.

2   These are the closing lines of Goethe's poem 'Natur und Kunst'
    ('Nature and Art'), translator's translation.

3   Official figures show that 14 per cent of Dutch children (one
    in seven) receive special care or special education, and that
    those measures are principally put in place to tackle less serious
    problems (Hermanns, 2009). I assume the figures for many
    Western countries will be in the same order of magnitude.

4   *Battle Hymn of the Tiger Mother* (2011) is a bestselling book by the
    US writer Amy Chua. See also http://amychua.com/

5   Home Office press release: 'Children Remind Adults To Act
    Responsibly on Our Streets', 4 April 2007, http://webarchive.
    nationalarchives.gov.uk/20091212125222/asb.homeoffice.gov.uk/
    news/article.aspx?id=10310

6   Pester power is a concept from the world of advertising: direct
    advertising for sweets and toys aimed straight at children, who will
    then nag their parents to buy the desired goods until the parents
    can't stand it anymore and eventually purchase the products in
    question. Furedi (2009) describes how this concept is now also
    being used by government agencies to improve parents' behaviour
    through their children.

7   The study in the Netherlands was carried out by MotivAction
    and was cited by Professor Jo Hermanns in a lecture that provides
    a nuanced picture of young people, and parents' view of them
    (Hermanns, 2009).

8   Furedi, 2009.

Chapter Two: Authority and Origin: 'Why? Because I say so!'

1   Authority has been studied for centuries, and from very many
    different perspectives. For readers looking for a solid historical
    overview, I recommend Furedi's *Authority* (2013). There are also
    some more recent studies on authority. Richard Sennett devoted a
    book to the subject in 1980. On education, see Furedi's 2009 work.
    The most personal study is that by Christien Brinkgreve (2012).
    As this chapter shows, Hannah Arendt's analysis offers the best
    way to understand the changes we are seeing in our time.

2   De la Boétie understands authority to be the absolute power of the
    rulers of his day (the 'Dictator' in the title of his essay). His claim
    is that we give those rulers their power (by voluntarily submitting
    to them), which also means we can take that power away from
    them.

3   Harari, 2011, ch. 8.

4 This is the message propagated by Thomas Insel, Chairman of the National Institute of Mental Health, an American institution that has had a worldwide impact on academic research. It was expressed in early 2013; see https://www.youtube.com/watch?v=u4m65sbqbhY. This lecture sounds convincing unless you know all the aspects Insel fails to mention (e.g. unquestioning acceptance among clinicians of the psychosocial causes of psychiatric disorders, and the lack of hard scientific evidence that psychiatric disorders are diseases of the brain).

5 Freud, 1953b and 1953a.

6 Freud, 1953g and 1953f.

7 Freud, 1953f.

8 The manuscript of *Pensées* was discovered in several loose fragments after Pascal's death. These fragments have been arranged and numbered differently by different editors. I follow the numbering of the Brunschvicg edition.

9 Harari, 2014, ch. 6.

10 My italics. This is the opening sentence of Kant's essay 'What is Enlightenment?' from the year 1784.

11 de Waal, 2013, ch. 6.

12 Rawls, 1971, ch. 3.

13 Derrida, 1992.

14 'Therefore we must assume that nature allows reconciliation between ... free will and the general law of liberty; and so we have found a natural law which allows the use of violence' (Kant, 1968; quoted by Ieven, 2005).

15 Blom, 2013.

16 Furedi, 2013, pp. 318–319; 327–331.

17 Arendt, 1954. Biography: Young-Bruehl, 1982.

18 The description of this appears at the end of Plato's *Republic*, in the Myth of Er — a fallen soldier who miraculously returns from the dead and recounts his experiences in the afterlife.

19 Pascal, 1958, no. 294.

20 Paleo-anthropologists believe patriarchal societies date back to the

time during the Neolithic when humans made the transition from a nomadic, hunter-gatherer lifestyle to a sedentary, agricultural way of life.

Chapter Three: Three Impossible Professions

1 Freud, 1953c and Lacan, 1984.
2 The Dutch television documentary series *Zembla* dedicated an entire program to this story: http://zembla.vara.nl/ seizoenen/2014/afleveringen/04-09-2014. Gotlieb's diary has now also been published (Gotlieb, 2014).
3 See https://en.wikipedia.org/wiki/Causa_Guttenberg
4 Lacan, 1992.
5 Carne Ross worked for many years as a high-ranking civil servant in the British diplomatic service, and was closely involved in the decisions leading to the war against Iraq. His experience led him to refute the belief that politicians have a better understanding of matters. In fact, the opposite is true, and their decisions often have disastrous consequences for the population. Information from locals is better, but is almost never acted upon. Ross has written a book whose radical proposal is that a 'leaderless society' is better off. The examples he gives are uncomfortably convincing. His book is a complement to Barbara Tuchman's historical study, *The March of Folly*, in which she shows how tragic the consequences of decisions made by political rulers can be.
6 Twelve per cent is the average for the European Union (cf. Laeven & Valencia, 2013).
7 The Netherlands Institute for Social Research, *Een beroep op de burger. Minder verzorgingsstaat, meer verantwoordelijkheid?* November 2012. Quoted and discussed by Luc Huyse, in his newspaper article 'Doe-het-zelf-samenleving', *De Standaard*, 2–3 August 2014. Luc Martens, the president of the Association of Flemish Cities and Municipalities, responded in the same newspaper, with a message that was even more pointed: yes, local governments can and will take on more responsibilities, but this

mustn't occur as part of a hidden strategy to shift the burden of funding cuts onto the citizens once again; furthermore, it must be accompanied by a process of *real* decentralisation, allowing local government to make their own decisions, without requiring them to increase in scale any further.

8 See http://stresscourse.tripod.com/id100.html and https://www. youtube.com/watch?v=RcGyVTAoXEU

9 LSE, 2006 and 2011.

10 The efficacy of 'evidence-based' psychotherapeutic treatments does appear to be a good bit lower in practice than the academic research would lead us to believe. I discussed the explanation for this in an essay (Verhaeghe, 2007). From a different perspective, this position was broadly confirmed by Moloney (2013).

11 Checking whether a therapy works is a good idea. Unfortunately, this type of 'quality control' (note the term: Who is the controller? Who is being controlled?) quickly evolved into a way of comparing therapists and facilities with each other, with the aim of making them 'more efficient'. In normal language: with the aim of making funding cuts. See Morrens, 2015.

Chapter Four: Return (Darth Vader) or Change (Big Brother)?

1 In a 2014 essay, Christien Brinkgreve described the same two trends. In her advice to the government, she is far more concrete than I am in this chapter, expressly emphasising improved communication in combination with expertise.

2 I would like to quote here a response to this paragraph sent to me by Ludo Couvreur in an email: 'It was Galileo who came up with the nice idea that "to experiment" was to ask questions of nature. Consequently, the answers will always remain answers to questions asked by people. Those questions are contained within a certain way of thinking and aimed at a particular goal. Objectivity consists of believing that answers can exist without questions having been asked, and results can exist independently of questioning. Now, it is also the case that we are overwhelmed by a mass of data. A

mass of data and conditions which are so intertwined and varied that it would be difficult to fit them all onto a graph with only two or three axes. As soon as we intervene in the statistics by asking a question, we make a selection and therefore discriminate against that which we do not select, that which we do not ask; as soon as we organise figures, we interfere with the world of disorder. In the economy, any data intervention is carried out post factum, and calculated predictability is reduced to unpredictability by human actions, which are intrinsically unpredictable. When you encrypt economic figures into an all-encompassing theory to explain the past and see its predictability as obligatory, the calculated prophecy becomes self-fulfilling, as is the case for any ideology. And when everything runs automatically, without any numbers, God is invoked, putting the figures right with his invisible hand. In the natural sciences, it is always nature itself which draws a veil over that which cannot be seen, just as other things are brought to light by a new discovery. Nature does its own thing, as if it were capable of human action itself. This is why numbers only stand up in relation to nature and people when the frame of reference is frozen. And the strangest thing that has been observed through measurement and figures comes from the field of quantum physics: the mere act of measuring something interferes with the result of that measurement, leaving you with an "uncertainty", to the great dismay of one of the greatest scientists of numbers, Einstein: "God does not play dice!" And yet, despite all that relativity, numbers have an effect on human achievements: technological progress — even insights in quantum physics — are perhaps the reason why numbers seem so magical. This is only the case because we then keep them "under control", forcing them to do our will. And this is also why any number that comes out of a computer needs to be interpreted in order for it to be useful to human beings. But continuing to question numbers, or what we imagine to be numbers, and why they appear, is indeed a source of richness.' See also https://doxaludo.wordpress.com/

3 The Swedish government carried out a more or less similar program with the same final results. In contrast to the British government, the Swedish government acknowledged the results and abandoned the program. This and other examples can be found in Moloney, 2013.

4 Figures are often incorrect, and the public are gradually beginning to realise this, thanks to the work of people like Andreas Tirez and Matthias Somers, who carefully examine the statistics quoted by politicians and don't hesitate to expose mistakes and deliberate deception. The fact remains that even figures that are 'correct' in the social context are determined by the questions they are put forward to answer. And this aspect still receives too little public attention.

5 See https://en.wikipedia.org/wiki/Phrases_from_The_ Hitchhiker%27s_Guide_to_the_Galaxy#Answer_to_the_ Ultimate_Question_of_Life.2C_the_Universe.2C_and_ Everything_.2842.29

6 Welzer, 2013. Before I'm pilloried by my fellow academics, let me hastily explain that scientific economics and psychology are indeed possible, provided that the appropriate methods are used, and those are not the methods of the exact sciences. One of the main requirements of the exact sciences is that of reproducibility, which means that when an experiment is repeated under the same conditions it should produce the same results. The speed at which an apple falls from a tree is the same everywhere, under the same conditions, and so Newton's law is indeed just that: a law. In the human sciences such as psychology and economics, experiments are almost never reproducible (which is why it is rarely attempted). The explanation for this is simple: they are not exact sciences, and the 'measurements' they make do not have the same standing. The investigation methods that are possible in the human sciences, and which can affect policy decisions, combine quantitative measurements with qualitative research. The most famous current example of this is the research carried out by Bent Flyvbjerg

(Oxford) — which should be required reading for all politicians; see http://www.sbs.ox.ac.uk/community/people/bent-flyvbjerg

7 I based this example on a study carried out by Mattias Desmet (2013). He shows that when a psychologist uses different kinds of instruments (for example a self-report questionnaire, a projective test, and a semi-structured interview) to measure the same psychological characteristic, the results will hardly ever agree.

8 Over-regulation goes hand in hand with an obsession with measuring. The illusion is that 'objective' figures will provide a foundation for yet more regulation. In practice, what these measurements usually lead to is simply yet more measurements.

The fifth and latest edition of the most widely used classification system in psychiatry, the *Diagnostic and Statistical Manual of Mental Disorders*, was published recently. The *DSM-5* is based on similar measurement procedures to those described in the previous endnote. In an inspired moment, the Belgian psychiatrist and psychoanalyst Hubert Van Hoorde coined the word 'statistiatry' for this. The difference between this and exact science is huge (but not measurable). What we can predict with certainty is that the number of disorders will continue to increase; more than 100 have been added to the manual since its previous edition. Grief is no longer grief, but a form of depression (so bring on the pills), the diagnostic criteria for ADHD have been broadened (yet more Ritalin), and the manual finally confirms what macho men have known all along: just before they get their period, women are mentally disturbed.

However, the American authors overlooked one of the most important mental illnesses of our time. This is no accident, since I suspect that most are suffering from it themselves, albeit without realising it (this lack of self-awareness means they also have another disorder: anosognosia). Since everyone has the right to a diagnosis these days, I propose a new label, fully in the style of the *DSM*. Following the trend for mind-numbing abbreviations, the label I have given this condition is PEED, or 'pseudo-efficiency and effectivity disorder'. These are the diagnostic criteria for PEED:

PSEUDO-EFFICIENCY AND EFFECTIVITY DISORDER

This diagnosis is attributed to individuals who display at least three of the following five characteristics:

A. The individual suffers from the delusion that everything can be measured and quantified, and is prone to outbursts of aggressive behaviour when corrected on this point.

B. The individual suffers from a compulsive need to register everything, in particular the behaviour and characteristics of others; only in extremely exceptional cases does the individual apply this to him- or herself.

C. The individual is extremely sensitive to change, and demands a completely predictable and standardised environment; even unimportant variations in this environment cause attacks of anxiety and/or rage. NB: This does not apply to the many changes introduced by the individual him- or herself.

D. The individual's use of language becomes increasingly incomprehensible, and no longer corresponds to any recognisable reality.

E. The individual suffers from megalomania and is convinced that his or her actions can only benefit the organisation to which he or she belongs.

This disorder is part of a broader group of anxiety disorders, highly contagious, and always damaging to the environment. So far, there is no efficient or effective

> treatment, but the pharmaceutical industry has set
> up a randomised controlled study of a new and very
> powerful antipsychotic drug.

9   Bauman & Lyon, 2013.

10 Serres, 2014 and Baricco, 2013.

11 Le Bon, 1895 and Freud, 1953e.

12 The idea of breaking with the traditional, rigid command structure appears, for example, in military training manuals. *Richtlinien für die Führung und Einsatz der Panzer-Division*, published in 1938, still included an organisational chart of command structure. From the 1940 edition onwards, this was removed (Dinardo, 2006, p. 119). I was made aware of the *Kampfgruppen* idea by ... a management book, in which the authors explicitly advocate for a move away from the American model and towards this European approach. I feel their work deserves more attention: Versnel & Brouwer, 2011. I've heard that some American companies are also now changing their approach. However: as long as such changes remain limited to introducing a few new human-resource management tricks, there'll be little real change. That's the lesson to be learned from the Semco model, which I discuss in chapter seven.

Chapter Five: The Age of Woman

1   The last witch-burning in Laarne, the Flemish village I live in, took place in 1607.

2   Translation quoted from *The New Yorker*, 17 August 2012. See http://www.newyorker.com/news/news-desk/the-pussy-riot-verdict

3   See http://www.popline.org/node/363769 and http://www.nocirc.org/symposia/first/hosken.html

4   The former Belgian national airline, Sabena, enforced an upper age limit for its stewardesses (they had to quit at 40). Gabrielle Dufrenne challenged her dismissal in court (in 1968, what a

coincidence!). It took almost ten years for the court to rule in her favour. The case was back on the political agenda as late as 2009. See https://en.wikipedia.org/wiki/Defrenne_v_Sabena_(No_2) and http://www.senate.be/www/?LANG=nl&LEG=4&MIval=/ Vragen/SchriftelijkeVraag&NR=2606

5 See http://ww.ugentmemorie.be/dossiers/ vrouwelijke-studenten-aan-de-ugent

6 OECD, 2011a.

7 Rosin, 2013.

8 Discussion of this issue is often ideological: on one side is a group of people who blame the problems faced by boys on the — in their view — regrettable decline in masculinity as a whole, by which they mean the patriarchy; on the other side is a group of people who tend to see this decline as progress.

9 For the figures in the US, see *The New York Times*, 17 February 2012. For Europe, see OECD, 2011b, p. 8 and p. 13. The 34 countries that belong to the OECD show more or less the same trends as in the West, together with Japan and South Korea.

10 For the increase in violence among women, see, Chesney-Lind, M. 'Girls and Violence: is the gender gap closing?', VAWnet, 2004 (quoted in Rosin, 2013). For social psychology research into the influence of social expectations, see Lightdale & Prentice, 1994.

11 It's not possible to ascertain the reliability of these figures; see http://www.slate.com/articles/news_and_politics/ foreigners/2009/06/the_herbivores_dilemma.html

12 Kathleen Bogle's (2008) research shows that 'hooking up' has replaced classic dating on American college campuses. What has not changed is that female students still risk being labelled a 'slut' (see an interview with Bogle: http://www.insidehighered. com/news/2008/01/29/hookups). Another study, which ran over a period of four years, shows among other things that pressure to pursue a career is detrimental to investing in long-term relationships and therefore promotes hooking-up behaviour (Hamilton & Armstrong, 2009).

13 Watch at http://www.npo.nl/3doc/14-11-2013/
    VPWON_1155462

14 Sennett, 2002, p. 7.

15 Hekma, 2004, p. 39.

16 OECD, 2011b.

17 For research on this phenomenon (by biological anthropologist
    Helen Fisher), see Rosin, 2013. For statistics concerning gender
    preference among American parents, see http://www.ingender.
    com/xyu/Gender-Preference/

18 The title of this adaptation of Aristophanes' *A Parliament of Women*
    was *Women at the Top*. See http://shc.stanford.edu/news/research/
    stanford-classics-theater-perform-women-top. Aristophanes'
    comedy has long been seen by male classicists as a warning *against*
    women in politics. The female students from Stanford see a very
    different message in it.

19 Young, 1958 and Gerzema & D'Antonio, 2013.

20 That companies run by women do better is the central position of
    an American research group, Catalyst (2004). Empirical evidence
    for this is rather limited, partly for the simple reason that there are
    still more men in leadership positions than women. For a nuanced
    discussion, see Marinova et al., 2010.

21 Social change concerning authority directly implies a change in
    the area of leadership, and this is happening apace in business.
    This can be seen from the following references: Washington, R.R.
    et al. 'How Distinct is Servant Leadership Theory?: empirical
    comparisons with competing theories', *Journal of Leadership,
    Accountability, and Ethics*, 2014, 11(1); Carson, J.B. et al. 'Shared
    Leadership in Teams: an investigation of antecedent conditions
    and performance', *Academy of Management Journal*, 2007, 50(5),
    pp. 1217–1234; Ashford, S. & DeRue, S. 'Leadership — It's
    (Much) More Than a Position', https://hbr.org/2010/04/
    leadership-its-much-more-than.html; DeRue, S. & Myers,
    C.G. 'Leadership Development: a review and agenda for future
    research' in: Day, D.V. (ed.) *The Oxford Handbook of Leadership and*

Organisations. Oxford: Oxford University Press, 2014; Pearce, C.L. & Sims, H.P. 'Vertical Versus Shared Leadership as Predictors of the Effectiveness of Change Management Teams: an examination of aversive, directive, transactional, transformational, and empowering leader behaviours', *Group Dynamics: Theory, Research, and Practice*, 2002, 6(2), pp. 172–197; Walumbwa, F.O. et al., 'Authentic Leadership: development and validation of a theory-based measure', *Journal of Management*, 2008, 34(1), pp. 89–126.

22 A week before the Institute for the Equality of Women and Men filed their complaint, an individual mother had already lodged a complaint (*De Standaard*, 21 November 2014). And on 29 May 2015, *De Standaard* published as its letter of the day 'Humiliated by the law', the story of a woman whose ex-partner refused to approve her application for a double-barrelled name for their child.

Chapter Six: Parents in the Plural

1 Pascal, 1958, no. 298.

2 Furedi, 2009, ch. 7.

3 This is the opening example in a critical study of modern psychology (De Vos, 2012). In his book with the telling title of *Wasted: why education isn't educating*, Frank Furedi rightly points out that the therapeutic turn in education goes hand in hand with the loss of classic pedagogical authority.

4 Furedi, 2009.

5 Omer, 2010. Even a limited search online shows the widespread interest in this approach. My interpretation of his 'old' authority as 'patriarchal' is not a misrepresentation of his account. I replaced the little word 'new' with 'collective' or 'shared' authority. 'New' will be outdated within a few years and doesn't indicate the intended meaning.

Chapter Seven: Your Money or Your Life

1 Max Weber (2009) was the first to make this comparison between capitalism and Christianity, in 1905. In 1921, Walter

Benjamin went a step further and called capitalism a religion in its own right, with the impossibility of full debt redemption as its central feature. 'This is a cult that engenders blame. Capitalism is presumably the first case of a blaming, rather than a repenting cult. Herein stands this religious system in the fall of a tremendous movement. An enormous feeling of guilt not itself knowing how to repent, grasps at the cult, not in order to repent for this guilt, but to make it universal ...' In modern terms: growth is a permanent requirement; debt is a permanent consequence. According to Benjamin, the endpoint is total despair. 'In the essence of this religious movement that is capitalism lies — bearing until the end, until the finally complete infusion of blame into God — the attainment of a world of despair still only hoped for.' This argument also applies to individuals. As managers of themselves, individuals must strive for ever-increasing efficiency, becoming increasingly exhausted in the process; even moments of rest have been abolished. 'The concretisation of the cult connects with a second characteristic of capitalism: the permanent duration of the cult. Capitalism is the celebration of the cult *sans [t]rêve et sans merci.* Here there is no "weekday", no day that would not be a holiday in the awful sense of exhibiting all sacred pomp — the extreme exertion of worship.'

2   See https://www.youtube.com/watch?v=MEaJYeRpl1g. The central character, Gordon Gekko (played by Michael Douglas), is a psychopathic stock trader and is intended by director Oliver Stone as a warning. However, he had precisely the opposite effect. Gekko became a role model for young Americans who were anxious to make it big. Another US movie, *American Psycho* (2000), was more successful in that respect.

3   This is why I see so-called microcredits as the precursor of 'free money'. The original idea was that lending small amounts of money to people who couldn't get credit from a normal bank would help them set up their own businesses. The originator of the idea, Muhammad Yunus, was awarded the 2006 Nobel Peace

Prize. Over time, this has turned out to be a continued success ... for the banks. The original funds are no longer sufficient, the banks have 'discovered' this market, and the interest they charge fluctuates between about 20 and 30 per cent (Hunter, 2011). And the result? Almost half the people who were previously just poor are now poor *and* in debt. The good news is that measures are being implemented to stop this abuse (Polgreen & Bajaj, 2010; Bajaj, 2011). Irrespective of their success or failure, this remains a micro-version of what we see happening on the macro-scale: companies, and even countries, whose 'economy' operates on a mountain of debt. 'Free money' (giving every adult a guaranteed basic income) is a better option.

4 In the space of barely three pages, Roubini, one of the few economists who accurately predicted the banking crisis, provides a very clear insight into the way modern credit-rating agencies work, and clearly outlines the changes that need to be made (Roubini & Mihm, 2010).

5 Reporting about unemployment figures often provides a beautiful illustration of the way supposedly objective figures can be manipulated. For example: compare the annualised number of unemployed people eligible for benefits today with the year that saw the highest unemployment figures. For Belgium that was 2004 and — surprise, surprise! — reports about unemployment figures often begin with the triumphant headline, 'Unemployment has fallen by x per cent since 2004'. You never read, 'Unemployment has risen by x per cent since 2008'. In 2008, Belgium saw its lowest unemployment figures since 2002. It takes some work to decipher the figures. Another trick is to 'creatively' change the criteria for registering someone as officially unemployed. So many different countries have done this in so many different ways that the OECD deemed it necessary to come up with its own measure: the Harmonised Unemployment Rate, or HUR. The fact is that we are moving inexorably towards much higher unemployment in the short term, due to the automation

of jobs in the mid-levels of society. No government can create enough jobs to absorb this effect. The sensible political response is to think radically about the redistribution of work. All the more so since there are now only two kinds of people: those with no work and those with too much.

6 *De Standaard*, 28 December 2012. In a discussion of Trudy Dehue's book *De depressie-epidemie*, E. Mortier noted the following: 'Suddenly, healthcare became about "care management", there was talk of "streamlining care profiles" and other obscurities wrapped up in so much plastic jargon. Caring for patients suddenly became "care operations", and the care manager measured how much time (and money) such an operation could (and should) cost. Treatment wards became unmoving conveyor belts, where ever decreasing numbers of healthcare workers hurried past ever increasing numbers of beds, in a kind of nursing which has much in common with modern auto assembly lines. This evolution was just one side of the overhaul of the post-war welfare state which had clearly wrapped us up in far too much cotton wool and made us too soft for the competition in the new global economy, where competition and individual efforts are stronger "assets" than cooperation and solidarity.' (*Standaard der Letteren*, 26 September 2008).

7 International Labour Organisation, 2015.

8 Mazzucato, 2013.

9 An incredible amount of research has been done on the way Iceland handled the crisis. My description is partly based on the Iceland Chamber of Commerce, *The Icelandic Economic Situation*, Status Report, 15th edition, April 2012. To gain a good idea of the activities surrounding the constitution, see Landemore, H. 'The Icelandic experience challenges the view that the constitutional process must be exclusionary and secretive', http://www.democraticaudit.com/2014/07/23/ the-icelandic-experience-challenges-the-view-that-constitutional-process-must-be-exclusionary-and-secretive/, based on 'Inclusive

Constitution-Making: the Icelandic experiment', *Journal of Political Philosophy*, 2014, 23(2). On Icesave, see Parker, I. 'Lost, after Financial Disaster, Icelanders Reassess Their Identity', 29 March 2009, *The New Yorker*, http://www.newyorker.com/magazine/2009/03/09/lost-19

10 On the cause of the Amazon.com boycott, see http://www.independent.co.uk/news/world/europe/amazon-used-neo-nazi-guards-to-keep-immigrant-workforce-under-control-in-germany-8495843.html. On child labour in Indian quarries, see http://www.flanderstoday.eu/business/local-cobblestones-linked-child-labour. On tax avoidance by Starbucks, see http://www.reuters.com/article/2012/10/15/us-britain-starbucks-tax-idusbre89e0ex20121015; and on how the subsequent customer boycott eventually forced the company to back down, see http://www.mirror.co.uk/news/uk-news/starbucks-move-hq-uk-pay-3419675 and http://www.dailymail.co.uk/news/article-2606274/Starbucks-pay-tax-Britain-relocates-European-headquarters-London-following-customer-boycott.html

11 There's a great deal of information available about Semco and Semler, starting with Wikipedia. Those who want to know more should read his book (1993) for themselves.

12 Harari (2011) refers to studies of indigenous South American tribes in this context. Violence is also a significant cause of death among the Kalahari Bushmen (Konner, 1984, p. 9). Rousseau's 'noble savage' is not so noble after all.

13 de Walsche, 2010 and Peeters, 2014.

14 Marinaleda is a village in Spain that's run as a cooperative, and which has attracted a lot of attention since the last economic crisis.

15 The information about Buurtzorg is taken in the first instance from an interview with Jan Rotmans (2013). Judging by modern-day indicators (profit, growth, customer and staff satisfaction), Buurtzorg is doing extremely well. Its CEO (Jos de Blok) is not a manager at all, but someone who inspires teams and lets them do their own thing. There are many online articles and documentaries

about the success of Mondragon. Wouter Torfs has written a book about his approach (2014). An informative interview about Frank Van Massenhove's approach can be found here: http://www.jandezutter.be/home/Interview_met_Frank_Van_Massenhove.html (in Dutch).

16 The internet is a very important tool for sharing. There are far too many examples to list, and not all examples are of commons/cooperatives. People share all sorts of goods and services, rooms, and transport. In addition, there are huge numbers of specific initiatives, ranging from sharing or exchanging toys, clothes, jewellery, and food, to joint use of buildings and gardens. The new architecture is moving more and more in this direction. In all of these examples there's an unmistakable shift away from single ownership and towards sharing, with the internet as a powerful facilitator, and with a strong focus on sustainability. One fascinating development in this context is the rise of digital 'currencies', often based on the amount of time spent providing a service for someone else, which can be used to 'buy' another person's time — 'time is money' takes on a literal meaning in this context.

17 The best-known of these are TripAdvisor and Yelp, but this area is also developing fast. New apps are constantly being released that allow users to simply scan a product with their smartphone and immediately see reviews from people who have bought that item — reviews that almost always refute misleading advertising claims. This is the latest form of social control and therefore of authority; you might say, an economic equivalent of WikiLeaks.

Chapter Eight: Mr Valdemar or Deliberative Democracy

1 van Bezien, et al., 2012.

2 For information on voter turnout in European elections, see http://www.europarl.europa.eu/elections2014-results/en/turnout.html

3 *De Standaard*, 3 August 2013. The writer David Van Reybrouck summarised this pithily: 'The coalition agreement is an ignoring

agreement' (*De Standaard*, 11 December 2014). See also https://
nl-nl.facebook.com/permalink.php?story_fbid=760734490668855
&id=266204043455238

4 In the words of the Louvain-based philosopher Thomas Decreus
(2013), 'democracy is not a state, but a movement which never
reaches a destination. It is a continuous process which endeavours
to neutralise inequalities of power.' See also Ieven, 2005.

5 OECD, 2015. The scientific evidence for the negative effects of
inequality has increased since the pioneering work of Wilkinson
& Pickett (2010). It continues to astound me how few people
are aware of this. One of the most renowned scientific journals,
Science, dedicated an entire issue to this, on 23 May 2014. See
http://www.sciencemag.org/site/special/inequality/

6 *De Standaard*, 16 June 2015.

7 Dabla-Norris et al., 2015. According to the IMF, the main
explanation for the increase in inequality is talent-based bonuses
— that is, the meritocracy. When I presented this explanation
in my book *What about Me?*, I was dismissed by many self-
proclaimed 'very important people' as incompetent and ignorant. I
would be interested to know if they feel the same about the IMF's
credentials.

8 Benjamin, 1976.

9 Gribnau, 2013.

10 For more on LuxLeaks, see https://www.theguardian.com/
business/2014/nov/05/-sp-luxembourg-tax-files-tax-avoidance-
industrial-scale. See also Maus, 2014.

11 For a report on this, see https://www.icij.org/project/swiss-leaks

12 An article by Fishkin himself explains nicely how this works. See
http://bostonreview.net/james-fishkin-nation-in-a-room-turning-
public-opinion-into-policy. For information on where and how
his model has already been applied, see http://cdd.stanford.edu.
For an extensive report on the British example, see http://cdd.
stanford.edu/2010/final-report-power-2010-countdown-to-a-
new-politics/ and Garton Ash, 2010.

13 Imagine a highly complex version of Doodle, in which the aim
   is not just to fix a date for a meeting, but also to choose what
   should be on the agenda for that meeting. LiquidFeedback
   can be downloaded free from the internet. It's one of the many
   examples of knowledge and the associated practice that have
   grown out of a collective whose first priority is to share. For more
   information, see https://en.wikipedia.org/wiki/LiquidFeedback
   and http://techpresident.com/news/wegov/22154/
   how-german-pirate-partys-liquid-democracy-works
14 Wilkinson & Pickett, 2010.

Conclusion

1 Spontaneous prosocial behaviour in young children was studied
  by Warneken & Tomasello (2009) of the Max Planck Institute,
  and their results have repeatedly been confirmed. See http://
  www.parentingscience.com/helpful-kids-and-rewards.html. These
  results find even broader validation in practically all of Frans
  de Waal's sociobiological research. One example appeals to the
  imagination: primates (viz. us) display an innate reaction against
  unfairness (for a video that is both convincing and hilarious, see
  https://www.youtube.com/watch?v=meiU6TxysCg). What's
  striking about the results of research into prosocial behaviour in
  small children is the extent to which allowing them to decide
  for themselves (rather than being forced to share with others by
  well-meaning parents, for example) increases their spontaneous
  helpfulness, and vice versa. This preference for autonomy and
  its positive implications have been discovered by a new field of
  research in psychology known as self-determination theory. It's
  no accident that this theory is currently enjoying a great deal of
  success. It strikes a chord with the spirit of our times.